19.20

920
LAKERS

OA

33971

MW01610897

DATE DUE

4-29-10		

GREAT SPORTS TEAMS

OAK FOREST HIGH SCHOOL--IMC

THE LOS ANGELES LAKERS

JOHN F. GRABOWSKI

Lucent Books, San Diego, CA

On Cover: Shaquille O'Neal and Hakeen Olajuwon

Library of Congress Cataloging-in-Publication Data

Grabowski, John F.
    The Los Angeles Lakers / by John F. Grabowski.
        p. cm.—(Great sports teams)
Includes bibliographical references (p.) and index.
Summary: Discusses the history of the Lakers basketball
team and the lives and careers of players George Mikan,
Elgin Baylor, Jerry West, Kareem Abdul-Jabbar, Magic
Johnson, Pat Riley, and Shaquille O'Neal.
    ISBN 1-56006-942-2 (alk. paper)
    1. Los Angeles Lakers (Basketball team)—History—
Juvenile literature. 2. Basketball players—United
States—Biography—Juvenile literature. [1. Los Angeles
Lakers (Basketball team)—History. 2. Basketball—
History.] I. Title. II. Series.
    GV885.52.L67 G73   2002
    796.323'64'0979494—dc21

2001004292

Copyright © 2002 by Lucent Books, Inc.
10911 Technology Place, San Diego, CA 92127
Printed in the U.S.A.

Contents

FOREWORD

Former Supreme Court Chief Justice Warren Burger once said he always read the sports section of the newspaper first because it was about humanity's successes, while the front page listed only humanity's failures. Millions of people across the country today would probably agree with Burger's preference for tales of human endurance, record-breaking performances, and feats of athletic prowess. Although these accomplishments are far beyond what most Americans can ever hope to achieve, average people, the fans, do want to affect what happens on the field of play. Thus, their role becomes one of encouragement. They cheer for their favorite players and team and boo the opposition.

ABC Sports president Roone Arledge once attempted to explain the relationship between fan and team. Sport, said Arledge, is "a set of created circumstances—artificial circumstances—set up to frustrate a man in pursuit of a goal. He has to have certain skills to overcome those obstacles—or even to challenge them. And people who don't have those skills cheer him and admire him." Over a period of time, the admirers may develop a rabid—even irrational—allegiance to a particular team. Indeed, the word "fan" itself is derived from the word "fanatic," someone possessed by an excessive and irrational zeal. Sometimes this devotion to a team is because of a favorite player; often it's because of where a person lives, and, occasionally, it's because of a family allegiance to a particular club.

Whatever the reason, the bond formed between team and fan often defies reason. It may be easy to understand the appeal of the New York Yankees, a team that has gone to the World Series an incredible 37 times and won 26 championships, nearly three times as many as any other major league baseball team. It is more difficult, though, to comprehend the fanaticism of Chicago Cubs fans, who faithfully follow the progress of a team that hasn't won a World Series since 1908. Regardless, the Cubs have surpassed the 2 million mark in home attendance in 14 of the last 17 years. In fact, their two highest totals were posted in 1999 and 2000, when the team finished in last place.

Each volume in Lucent's *Great Sports Teams* series examines a team that has left its mark on the American sports consciousness. Each book looks at the history and tradition of the club in an attempt to understand its appeal and the loyalty—even passion—of its fans. Each volume also examines the lives and careers of people who played significant roles in the team's history. Players, managers, coaches, and front office executives are represented.

Footnoted quotations help bring the text in each book to life. In addition, all books include an annotated bibliography and a Further Reading list to supply students with sources for conducting additional individual research.

No one volume can hope to explain fully the mystique of the New York Yankees, Boston Celtics, Dallas Cowboys, or Montreal Canadiens. The Lucent *Great Sports Teams* series, however, gives interested readers a solid start on the road to understanding the mysterious bond that exists between modern professional sports teams and their devoted followers.

Showtime!

A side from the Boston Celtics, no National Basketball Association (NBA) team has a richer tradition of showmanship and a more glorious past than the Los Angeles Lakers. From the time of the club's inception more than a half century ago in the northern climes of Minnesota, only the Boston Celtics have won more league championships—sixteen to the Lakers' twelve. If appearances in the Championship Series are measured competitively, the Lakers triumph. They have lost thirteen times in the final round, for a total of twenty-five appearances; the Celtics have lost three times, for a runner-up total of nineteen.

Since moving west in 1960, the Lakers have become one of the most visible franchises in professional sports. An endless stream of celebrities flock to the Los Angeles Forum to watch the top stars in the game ply their talents. During Magic Johnson's career, his passion for the game was obvious to all who saw him play. His charming, flashy enthusiasm was transmitted to his teammates and promoted by the media, giving rise to the term "Showtime!"

The Lakers have never lacked for star players. Some of the greatest players ever to lace up a pair of sneakers have worn Laker jerseys at some time in their careers. In addition to the aforementioned Johnson, the list includes George Mikan, Elgin Baylor, Jerry West, Kareem Abdul-Jabbar, Magic Johnson, and Shaquille O'Neal.

As much as any team, the Lakers' popularity has been responsible for helping the NBA attain status as a full-fledged major sports league. George Mikan's presence in the late 1940s helped

One of basketball's greatest players, Wilt Chamberlain, joins the list of Laker stars.

establish the sport at the professional level. Prior to that time, the college game was more popular with the sporting public. The team's move to California in 1960 established the game in a whole new market. Twenty years later, Magic Johnson, together with Boston's Larry Bird, revitalized the pro game and helped the league obtain a lucrative television contract. Fans watched with dedication as arguably the two greatest all-around players of the day led their respective teams to the League Championship Series year after year.

The present-day Lakers are again the league's dominant team. Shaquille O'Neal and Kobe Bryant are helping to carry on the club's winning tradition. Their championships in 2000 and 2001 give every indication that "Showtime!" is still on top as the new millennium unfolds.

CHAPTER 1

From the Land of Lakes

To many, southern California seems like a dream. The beautiful weather, glistening beaches, and bustling tourist attractions make it a popular vacation spot, almost a modern fantasy world. Adding to the illusion are the television and movie personalities who call Los Angeles home. With entertainment stars living among them, it should be no surprise that Californians desire larger-than-life sports heroes as well, which accounts for a good part of the Los Angeles Lakers' popularity and success over the years. Players like Elgin Baylor, Magic Johnson, and Shaquille O'Neal have performed seemingly supernatural athletic feats in the entertainment capital of the world. Interestingly enough, the Lakers' superstar tradition extends back to the early days of the team's existence, far removed from the glitz and glamour of its current home.

The Chicago American Gears

In 1947 major league sports were an unknown commodity in the state of Minnesota. Baseball's Twins and football's Vikings would not be established for another fourteen years. Pro basketball was a regional phenomenon, not yet national in scope. Into this professional sports void stepped local sportswriter Sid Hartman, who came up with the idea of bringing pro basketball to "The Land of 10,000 Lakes."

To test if a market for the sport existed, Hartman persuaded businessman Benjamin J. Berger to promote a local exhibition game between the Oshkosh and Sheboygan clubs of the National Basketball League (NBL). Established in 1937, the NBL was a pro league centered in the Midwest. The game drew five thousand fans and sparked Berger's interest in Hartman's plan.

Upon doing research, Hartman found that the Detroit Gems franchise in the NBL was struggling financially. With a 4–40 record and last-place finish the year before, the Gems were on the verge of collapse. The team's players, in fact, had already been assigned to other clubs in the league. Berger and local promoter Morris Chalfen raised $15,000 and sent Hartman to Detroit to purchase the franchise from owner Morris Winston on July 6, 1947. The new owners received little more than two sets of uniforms and the right to field a team.

Berger and Chalfen hired Max Winter as general manager and thirty-one-year-old John Kundla as coach. Kundla had been a star player first at Minneapolis' Central High School, then at the University of Minnesota. In an effort to give the team even more local flavor, former Minnesota Gophers Tony Jaros, Don Carlson, Don Smith, Warren Ajax, and Ken Exel were signed to contracts for the first season. Winter also signed former Stanford all-American Jim Pollard, who had been playing for an Amateur Athletic Union (AAU) team for the previous two years. The player who would make the franchise a success, however, was George Mikan, basketball's first true superstar.

After dominating the game at DePaul University, the six-foot, ten-inch Mikan signed a contract with the NBL's Chicago American Gears in 1946. The big man (his height was relatively rare for a player in the 1940s) helped the team win the league championship in his very first season of 1946–47. Following that season, Gears' owner Maurice White pulled his team out of the league. He visualized himself as the owner of a new twenty-four-team professional circuit, financing the enterprise with his personal fortune. His Chicago team, naturally, would be the centerpiece of his Professional Basketball League of America, headed by basketball's biggest drawing card, George Mikan.

Unfortunately for White, his league collapsed within weeks. Players from the Gears were distributed among the NBL's remaining teams. Because the Minneapolis club had the worst record in the league the previous year (as the Detroit Gems), they were given first pick. Their selection, naturally, was Mikan.

The League's First Dynasty

The team then known as the Minneapolis Lakers (named for the large cargo-carrying ships that passed through the nearby Great Lakes) quickly jumped into the upper echelon of the NBL standings with a 43–17 record. Playing most of their home games in the Minneapolis Auditorium, the Lakers won the league title, defeating the Rochester Royals in the best-of-five final series. They ended the year with a victory in the last World Professional Tournament, a competition for professional teams started by the Chicago *Herald-American* newspaper in 1939.

At the same time, the Basketball Association of America (BAA)—a new league with franchises in several large eastern cities—had just completed its second season of play. The NBL had better players and stronger teams than the upstart league, but its teams played in smaller arenas in smaller towns. BAA president Maurice Podoloff saw the benefits of a merger with the older circuit and persuaded four NBL teams to jump to the BAA. On May 10, 1948, the Lakers, Fort Wayne Zollner Pistons, Indianapolis Kautskys, and Royals each paid a $25,000 entry fee to join the league.

Despite the switch from the older, more established league, the Mikan-led Lakers still dominated and won the

George Mikan became basketball's first superstar.

1948–49 title. Mikan rewrote the record book, scoring a record 47 points in a December contest against the Chicago Stags. He posted 53 against the Baltimore Bullets less than three months later, but in the interim, Joe Fulks of the Philadelphia Warriors shattered Mikan's mark by pouring in 63 against the Indianapolis Jets. Mikan's season total of 1,698 points was also a new league record.

The depleted NBL managed to continue to play that season, but the next year a merger was finalized. The new seventeen-team organization became known as the National Basketball Association (NBA). The NBA today dates its inception back to the BAA's first season of 1946–47.

The Lakers made three important additions to their team through the college draft that year. Guards Slater Martin and Bob Harrison, and center Vern Mikkelsen joined Mikan and Pol-

---

A portrait of the Minneapolis Lakers, basketball's first dynasty.

lard to form a strong nucleus for an emerging dynasty. With Mikan a fixture at center, the six-foot, seven-inch Mikkelsen was forced to switch positions, becoming the sport's first "power forward" (a forward whose main job—because of his physical size and strength—is preventing opposing players from getting close to the basket, as opposed to one who concentrates on scoring or playmaking). The club sailed to its third consecutive title, defeating the Syracuse Nationals in a physical six-game championship series. Following a one-year hiatus, the Lakers won three more titles in a row, giving them a run of six in seven years. The club was led to victory by its dominating front line. As basketball commentator John Devaney wrote, "standing shoulder to shoulder, Mikan, Mikkelsen and Pollard looked like a ragged row of alpine mountains."[1]

One of the Lakers' great rivalries of this early period in their history was with the barnstorming Harlem Globetrotters. (Barnstormers were teams that did not belong to any organized league, but rather eked out an existence by playing teams in different parts of the country.) Unlike the Globies of today—a team that entertains with bloopers and stunts rather than competing professionally—the team of the late '40s and early '50s concentrated on playing serious basketball. In 1948 the two clubs were pro basketball's two best teams. To take advantage of their superiority, general manager Max Winter came up with the idea of having the teams play each other in an annual series. The Globetrotters won the initial contest in 1948, then again in a rematch a year later. A second game that season was won by the Lakers, as were the four games played over the next three years. Globetrotters' owner Abe Saperstein eventually canceled the series after the January 1952 meeting as the Globies began placing more and more emphasis on entertaining the fans.

The Globetrotters were not the only team finding it difficult to beat Minneapolis. As the league's perennial champions, the Lakers were marked men. Opposing squads used every strategy imaginable to stop the Minneapolis juggernaut. In an attempt at quieting those who said that Mikan's size made it too easy for him to score, the league experimented by using twelve-foot-high baskets (rather than the standard ten-foot-high baskets) in a league game between the Lakers and Milwaukee Hawks. Some observers did not believe this was the answer. "Seems to me," wrote Minneapolis *Tribune* sportswriter Dick Cullum, "the higher basket will hurt the little fellow more than the tall one."[2] He was correct. As Lakers forward Mikkelsen explained, "It didn't help the smaller guy. It helped me—the big, strong rebounder, because it gave me another tenth of a second to get set after a shot."[3] The Lakers came out on top by a score of 65–63, with Mikkelsen leading the way for Minneapolis with 17 points.

The rough-and-tumble play and constant double-teams proved wearing on Mikan, who announced his retirement following the 1954 season. The team remained competitive for a while, but when Pollard retired the following year, the club's fortunes plummeted. Mikan briefly came out of retirement but could not reverse the losing trend.

As the Lakers' performance dropped, so, too, did attendance. The club had always been handicapped by no permanent home arena. It played most of its home games in the Minneapolis Auditorium. When games conflicted with more lucrative events, the team was forced to switch venues to the Minneapolis Armory, the St. Paul Auditorium, or the Norton Fieldhouse on the campus of Hamline University in St. Paul.

The lack of a permanent home court was just one of the factors that made Ben Berger seriously consider selling the team to Milton Fischman and former major league baseball shortstop Marty Marion. The pair intended moving the franchise to Kansas City, Missouri. However, a group of thirty individuals headed by local trucking magnate Robert E. Short, president of the Mueller Transit Company, joined together to purchase the club for $150,000, thereby keeping it in Minneapolis.

New ownership did not change the Lakers' fortunes. The team finished the 1958 season with the league's worst record. By doing so, however, they put themselves in line to select first in the annual college draft. With that number-one pick, they selected Elgin Baylor of Seattle University, generally recognized as the top college player.

The Lakers finished with a record below .500 in 1958–59, which included a franchise-record eleven straight losses in January. Sparked by Baylor, however, they made it all the way back to the championship round of the playoffs, eventually losing to the

Boston Celtics—an occurrence that would become an annoying annual rite of spring.

The Move West

Following the 1958–59 season, Mikkelsen retired and Coach Kundla left the Lakers to take over as head coach at the University of Minnesota. Under John Castellani and then Jim Pollard, the Lakers concluded the 1959–60 season with their second-worst mark ever—25–50. Because of the NBA's playoff structure, however

Despite Mikan's impressive presence on the court, the Lakers lost four seasons in a row before moving west.

(only two of the eight teams in the league did not qualify for the playoffs), the team was able to advance to the Western Division Finals, where they lost to the St. Louis Hawks (who had relocated from Milwaukee), four games to three.

Minneapolis fans were not fooled by the team's performance in the playoffs. Having been spoiled by the teams of the Mikan era, they had no interest in a squad that could not win even half their games. The future did not look promising. With baseball's Twins and football's Vikings beginning play in 1961, the Lakers would no longer be the only game in town. A period of urban decline in downtown Minneapolis added to the problem, as the area became less attractive to visitors.

Owner Robert Short had watched with interest two years earlier when the Brooklyn Dodgers and New York Giants abandoned the East Coast and moved to California. The financial potential offered by this untapped market was too great to pass up. On April 27, 1960, the league granted permission for Short to follow suit—the Lakers would move to Los Angeles for the 1960–61 season.

By the time the Lakers were ready to begin play their first season on the West Coast, they had added another weapon to their arsenal. Having compiled the second-worst record in the league the previous year, they were entitled to the second overall pick in the annual draft. After the Cincinnati Royals (the team moved from Rochester to Cincinnati in 1957) chose Oscar Robertson with the first selection, the Lakers followed by taking all-American guard Jerry West of the University of West Virginia.

Short hired West's college coach, Fred Schaus, as the Lakers' new head man. After a slow start of mixing the new players with the veterans, the team began to gel in the second half of the season. Led by Baylor and West, the Lakers showed an eleven-game improvement over the previous year, and made it as far as the Western Division Finals of the playoffs before they were stopped by the St. Louis Hawks in seven games. It would be the first of many frustrating moments for Laker teams of the 1960s.

A String of Near Misses

The Lakers made it to the top of the Western Division in 1961–62, finishing with a record of 54–26. After beating the Detroit Pistons in the division finals, they lost to Red Auerbach's Boston Celtics in an exciting seven-game series for the league title. In one of the most memorable championship games of all time, Boston won in overtime, as Lakers guard Frank Selvy's last-second shot skipped off the rim as the buzzer sounded to end regulation time.

The near miss would become a regular habit with the Lakers. They lost to the Celtics in the NBA Finals again four times between 1963 and 1968. By this time, Short had sold the team for $5 million to California industrialist Jack Kent Cooke. The sale positioned the league on a whole new economic level. The purchase price was comparable to that for which major league baseball teams were being sold. Cooke began to pour money into the team, and the look of the Lakers began to change.

The 1968–69 season was a note-worthy time in Lakers' history. They opened the doors to the Great Western Forum that owner

Wilt Chamberlain was to be the Lakers' match for Boston Celtics' Bill Russell.

Cooke had built to replace the Los Angeles Sports Arena that had been the Lakers' home. The club also unveiled new gold and purple uniforms to replace their old white and blue ones. The most significant decision of all concerned the makeup of the team. Cooke concluded that the Lakers would never be able to compete with the Celtics unless they had someone who could match up well with Boston's great center, Bill Russell. The one player who fit those qualifications was Wilt Chamberlain of the Philadelphia 76ers.

At the time, Chamberlain was in the midst of a salary contract dispute with 76ers' management. Cooke arranged a trade that brought Chamberlain to the Lakers in exchange for Jerry Chambers, Archie Clark, and Darrall Imhoff. With the big man added to a starting lineup that already included all-stars Baylor and West, reasoned Cooke, the Lakers would be unbeatable.

Los Angeles finished first in the Western Division that year while Boston could do no better than place fourth in the Eastern Division. When the two teams met in the championship series, however, the result was still the same. The Lakers won the first two games, but the Celtics fought back to even the series. With the final contest scheduled to be played in Los Angeles, Cooke had balloons suspended from the ceiling in the Forum in anticipation of a Los Angeles victory. Unfortunately, the celebration was not to be. The Celtics won the game, 108–106, sending the Lakers down to defeat one more time.

Back to the Top

The Lakers returned to the NBA Finals again in 1969–70, but this time their opponent was the New York Knicks. When New York's star center, Willis Reed, went down with a knee injury in Game 5, it appeared that the Lakers' luck had finally turned. With a magnificent team effort, however, the Knicks came back in the fourth quarter to win the game. Los Angeles won Game 6 to even the series at three games apiece, but Reed's inspirational return in the last contest sparked New York to victory and the championship.

Two years later, the Knicks and Lakers met for the title once again. This time, however, the Lakers lived up to their advance notices. Chamberlain sacrificed his scoring for the betterment of the team, concentrating instead on rebounding and setting up his teammates, and the results were spectacular. The Lakers put together a record thirty-three-game winning streak on their way to compiling a 69–13 mark. After losing the first game of the final series to the Knicks, Los Angeles came back to win the next four in a row for their first championship since moving West.

It would be the high point of the decade for the Lakers. They finished in first place in the Pacific Division in each of the next two seasons, but were clearly showing their age. In 1974–75, they finished with the next-to-worst record in the league. By that time, both Chamberlain and West had retired. The Lakers missed making the postseason for the first time in seventeen years, but help was on the way.

Milwaukee Bucks center Kareem Abdul-Jabbar, the predominant big man of the day, had demanded a trade, requesting a move to either New York or Los Angeles. In June 1975 the Bucks accommodated him, sending him to the Lakers in exchange for four players. He paid immediate dividends for Los Angeles, leading the team back into the playoffs, and winning the league's Most Valuable Player (MVP) award in each of his first two seasons with the club. By the end of the decade, the Lakers were ready to reclaim their position among the league's elite teams.

It's Showtime!

The final winning ingredient was added in the 1979 draft. The Lakers had the first overall pick as a result of compensation they received from the New Orleans Jazz for signing free agent guard Gail Goodrich. With that pick, they selected six-foot, nine-inch point guard Earvin "Magic" Johnson of Michigan State.

By this time, Cooke had sold the team and the Forum—along with the Los Angeles Kings hockey team and a thirteen thousand-acre California ranch—to real estate developer Jerry Buss for $67.5 million. Buss was determined to do whatever was necessary to make his team the showpiece of the league. He fired the Forum's organist and hired a band to excite the fans with music. He hired Laker girls to cheer for the team at courtside. He invited celebrities to the games, making stargazing part of the Laker experience. Gradually, the club became an integral part of the Hollywood entertainment scene. "I tried to create a Laker image, a distinct identity," Buss said. "I think we were successful. The Lakers are pretty damn Hollywood."[4]

Johnson and Abdul-Jabbar helped develop that image with their charisma and star quality. The new owner's first season was a rousing success as Kareem won his sixth—and final—MVP award, and Johnson made an electrifying debut. Magic was named the MVP of the NBA Finals as the Lakers defeated the Philadelphia 76ers for the title, and solidified their status as the glamour team of the NBA.

During the 1980s, the Lakers were the NBA's dominant club. Johnson directed them to four league titles (1982, 1985, 1987, 1988) and three other appearances in the finals series (1983, 1984, 1989). The club came under the guiding hand of Pat Riley, whom Buss

Coach Pat Riley led the Lakers to seven championships in nine years.

hired shortly after the start of the 1981–82 season. With his hair slicked back, the Armani-clad Riley added to the Hollywood image Buss was trying to establish. The only seasons in Riley's nine-year run in which the Lakers failed to reach the championship series were in 1986, when they were upset by the Houston Rockets in the Western Conference Finals, and in 1990 when they lost to the Phoenix Suns in the Conference Semifinals.

The Lakers' glorious run (which included nine straight division titles) was brought to an end through a combination of circumstances. Abdul-Jabbar retired following the 1988–89 campaign and Riley stepped down as coach a year later. The biggest blow of all, however, came in November 1991 when Magic Johnson announced his retirement after having tested positive for human immunodeficiency virus (HIV), the virus that leads to acquired immune deficiency syndrome (AIDS). Although he did make a brief comeback, his departure marked the end of an era, and a period of unparalleled growth for the entire league.

The post-Johnson years saw Michael Jordan and the Chicago Bulls dominate the NBA scene. The Lakers' fortune dropped to a low point in the mid-1990s, with the team bottoming out in 1993–94 with a record of 33–49. They began rebuilding, with Nick Van Exel, Eddie Jones, and Vlade Divac leading the way.

Two dramatic moves made prior to the 1996–97 season significantly sped up the process. Seven-foot, one-inch Orlando Magic center Shaquille O'Neal was signed by the Lakers as a free agent. Perhaps just as significant, the Lakers selected eighteen-year-old Kobe Bryant directly from high school in the annual college draft.

The Lakers selected eighteen-year-old Kobe Bryant in the 1996 college draft.

With O'Neal and Bryant leading the way, Los Angeles began to
make its way back to the league's upper echelon of teams. The final piece of the dazzling puzzle was added, when in June 1999
former Chicago Bulls' head coach Phil Jackson signed a $30 mil-
lion, five-year contract to coach the club.

In 1999–2000, the Lakers completed their journey back to the top
of the NBA in their new home, the Staples Center. After finishing
first in the Pacific Division of the Western Conference, they made
their way to the finals series where they met the Indiana Pacers.
The Lakers defeated Indiana in a hard-fought six-game series to
win their twelfth NBA crown. With O'Neal and Bryant aided by a
strong supporting cast, the Lakers began the new millennium with
the core of a new powerhouse securely in place.

CHAPTER 2

George Mikan

With his thick, dark glasses, George Mikan looked more like an accountant than an athlete. It is no exaggeration, however, to say that this gentle-looking giant saved the National Basketball Association. He was directly responsible for several rule changes that helped the game evolve into its present state. His popularity brought fans out at a time when the pro game was struggling to gain national attention. As *New York Post* columnist Milton Gross wrote when Mikan retired, "His presence made it possible for a game whose natural habitat was barrooms, barns and boxlike gyms to break out of its ghetto into the largest arenas in the land and take its place as a big-league professional sport."[5]

An Awkward Youth

George Lawrence Mikan Jr. was born on June 18, 1924, on a farm in Will County, near Joliet, Illinois. He was one of three sons born to parents of Balkan descent. Unlike many other sports heroes, he was not a star athlete as a youngster. He was tall, skinny, and awkward, and he wore glasses to correct his myopia (nearsightedness).

As a child, George's best game was marbles. When he was ten years old, he won the Will County championship, and with it, a

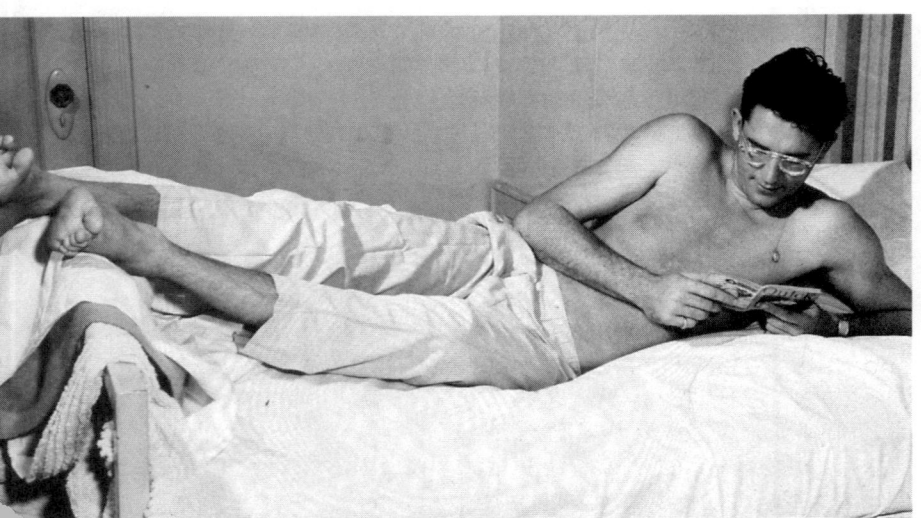

George Mikan grew up on a farm near Joliet, Illinois.

trip to Comiskey Park in Chicago to see the New York Yankees play the hometown White Sox. His biggest thrill was meeting Babe Ruth after the game and getting a home run ball autographed by the Bambino. "It was a terribly slow trip home," recalled Mikan. "I couldn't get home fast enough to show my Babe Ruth–autographed home-run ball to everybody."[6]

George's brothers, Ed (who would one day join George in the NBA ranks) and Joe, introduced him to the game of basketball, which they played in the backyard of their home in Joliet. George, however, showed more of a talent for baseball. He was one of the best sandlot pitchers in town and, like many youngsters, dreamed of someday playing in the major leagues.

When Mikan entered Joliet Catholic High School, he tried out for the basketball team as a freshman but was snubbed. "You can't play with glasses on,"[7] said the coach, killing the youngster's hopes. George temporarily gave up the sport and turned his attention to his schoolwork. He left Joliet Catholic and transferred to Quigley Preparatory Seminary in Chicago to study for the priesthood.

In his three years at Quigley, Mikan grew to six-feet, eight-inches tall. He had been playing basketball for a local Catholic

Youth Organization (CYO) team, but he suffered a severe compound fracture in his right leg, which hindered his progress. He played two or three games for the seminary's team in his last year at the school, by which time he had decided he had no calling for the priesthood.

Developing at DePaul

Mikan attracted the interest of both DePaul and Notre Dame because of his size and ability, despite his lack of experience on the basketball court. He was given a tryout at Notre Dame (allowable under the rules of the day), but failed to impress head coach George Keogan. Assistant Coach Ray Meyer, however, noticed his potential. "George did not have a good day," he said, "but it was a case of his just growing too fast and not playing much basketball. He was awkward. What he needed was some agility and finesse."[8]

Mikan eventually decided to enroll at DePaul. Meyer was hired as the school's head coach just two months later. He put George through a strenuous training regimen designed to help him improve his agility and dexterity. "I worked with that kid two to two-and-a-half hours every day," said Meyer. "I had him skip rope like a boxer. I brought in a coed to teach him to dance. . . . I did everything I could to improve his agility because I wanted a big guy like that playing for me."[9] One of the exercises, in which he threw up one hook shot after another from either side of the basket with either hand, became known as the Mikan drill.

Meyer's training strategy quickly paid off. Mikan began his sophomore season (1942–43) as the team's starting center. He scored 10 points in his first game and impressed everyone with his defense and shot-blocking. His scoring picked up as he validated Meyer's belief that "a big man could score more points by accident than a little one could trying hard."[10] He quickly showed his value to the team by leading DePaul to a 19–5 record and an invitation to the prestigious National Invitation Tournament (NIT) in New York.

By Mikan's junior season, he had perfected the art of goaltending (interfering with a shot while the ball is on its downward flight to the basket), which then was perfectly legal. As he recounted, "We would set up a zone defense that had four men around the key, and

I guarded the basket. When the other team took a shot, I'd just go up and tap it out."[11] Complaints became so loud that the National Collegiate Athletic Association (NCAA) Rules Committee changed the rule to make goaltending illegal. Mikan turned his energies toward offense, and he raised his scoring average to 18.7 points per game using his devastating hook shot. DePaul again made the postseason NIT and compiled a 22–4 mark for the year.

George Mikan forced the NCAA to make goaltending illegal.

In 1944–45, Mikan averaged 23.3 points per game to lead the nation in scoring. DePaul again made the NIT, this time winning the championship. Mikan set a tournament record by scoring 120 points in the three games, including an incredible 53 in the semifinal win over Rhode Island State. Since DePaul won that contest by a score of 97–53, Mikan scored as many points as Rhode Island all by himself.

In those days, NCAA rules allowed players one year of freshman ball and four years of varsity eligibility. In Mikan's last season, 1945–46, he again led the nation in scoring as DePaul went 19–5. For his four years, he averaged better than 19 points a game in leading the Blue Demons to 81 wins against only 17 defeats. He was a unanimous first team all-American in each of his last three years, and he was twice named College Player of the Year.

From Chicago to "Siberia"

At the time of Mikan's departure from DePaul, several professional leagues were vying for his attention.

Maurice White, owner of the American Gear Company and the Chicago American Gears of the NBL, immediately signed him to a five-year contract for the almost unheard of total of $62,000. The situation was ideal. The money would allow Mikan to continue working toward his law degree at DePaul.

Mikan proved to be as good as promised. Having signed after the conclusion of the college season, he could not participate in the team's regular season or playoff games. He was eligible, however, for the annual World Professional Tournament in Chicago. Removing all doubt as to whether he could play in the pro ranks, Mikan scored 100 points in five games, leading the Gears to the tournament semifinals. For his efforts, he was named the tournament's MVP.

A dispute over the terms of his contract caused Mikan to miss the first six weeks of the 1946–47 season. When he finally began playing, he averaged 16.5 points per game for twenty-five contests. He helped the Gears to the league title as they defeated the defending champion Rochester Royals.

Following the season, White pulled his team from the league and established his own twenty-four-team circuit—the Professional Basketball League of America. His grandiose scheme was short-lived, however. The league folded after only a month, White suffered a nervous breakdown, and the Chicago players were distributed among the eleven NBL teams in a reentry draft. The rights to Mikan were obtained by the first-year Minneapolis Lakers.

With his life centered around Chicago, Mikan did not look forward to playing in Minnesota. "I just got drafted by Siberia,"[12] he said. He had recently married Patricia Daveny, a young woman from Chicago, and he intended to keep working toward his law degree at DePaul. He agreed to meet with the owners of the Minneapolis franchise as a matter of courtesy, but he had no intention of signing with the team.

After making his intentions clear during final contract talks, Mikan asked to be driven to the airport for the flight home. The Minneapolis owners, however, were determined to do everything in their power to make him change his mind. As he later recalled, "I told them I would think about their offer. They were supposed to be taking me back to the airport. . . . We start driving around for

The Minneapolis Lakers signed George Mikan for $12,500 in 1946.

two hours, like they didn't know where the airport was. They finally found it, and by then, they wore me down. I signed with the Lakers."[13] His first contract with Minneapolis called for a salary of $12,500.

In Minneapolis, Mikan joined forces with former Stanford star Jim Pollard to form the nucleus of a budding dynasty. Led by the six-foot, ten-inch, 245-pound Mikan, nicknamed "Scaffold," the Lakers won the NBL Championship that season (1947–48). They also won the final World Professional Tournament, as Mikan scored 40 points in the championship game against the New York Rens, one of the dominant black teams of the day.

The next season, Minneapolis and three other NBL teams announced they were withdrawing from the league to join the upstart BAA. The change of leagues made little difference: Mikan won the scoring title and the Lakers again won the league championship. Mikan continued to be the league's top drawing card, as swarms of fans came out to see him score on his deadly hook shots. One winter's night in New York, the marquee at Madison Square Garden advertised a game with the Lakers by proclaiming, "GEO. MIKAN VS KNICKS." The sign did not escape the notice of his teammates. "I went into the locker room," said Mikan, recalling his teammates' joking reaction, "sat down, took off my glasses . . . and started to change into my uniform. I finished getting dressed, put my glasses back on, and the other guys were still sitting there in their street clothes. They looked at me and said, 'OK, big shot. You're supposed to play them. So go out and play them.' They razzed me for a long time."[14]

The marquee at Madison Square Garden read "Geo. Mikan vs. Knicks."

The NBA's First Dynasty

That summer, six surviving NBL teams joined forces with the BAA under the banner of the infant NBA. The new circuit opened the 1949–50 season with seventeen teams. The Lakers were assigned to the league's Central Division and finished the season with a 51–17 mark. Mikan dominated the league, leading in scoring with an average of 27.4 points per game. Only one other player in the league (Alex Groza of the Indianapolis Olympians) reached the 20-point level.

In the 1950 playoffs the Lakers swept past the Chicago Stags, Fort Wayne Pistons, and Anderson Packers in six straight games to reach the NBA Finals. There, they defeated the Syracuse Nationals in six games to win their third straight championship, each one in a different league. Mikan dominated, averaging better than 31 points a contest for the twelve postseason games. To put that into perspective, the Lakers' opponents averaged just 75 points per game.

The 1950–51 season marked the first year the NBA kept track of rebounds. In addition to leading once again in scoring, Mikan averaged more than 14 boards per game to finish second to Dolph Schayes of the Syracuse Nationals. The Lakers, however, had their streak of championships ended by the Rochester Royals, who defeated them in the Western Division Finals. Mikan averaged 24 points per game in the postseason, despite playing the Rochester series with a fractured leg. "The doctors taped a plate on it for the playoffs," said Mikan. "I played all right, scored in the 20s. I couldn't run, sort of hopped down the court." [15]

Rule Changes

On November 22, 1950, the Lakers and Fort Wayne Pistons played the lowest-scoring game in league history. The Pistons knew they were hopelessly overmatched by Minneapolis. They decided their only chance of winning was to try to neutralize Mikan by holding the ball and minimizing the number of shots that were taken. The strategy worked to perfection and the Pistons came out on top by a final score of 19–18.

Unfortunately, the game was a disaster from the fans' point of view. The NBA was trying to establish itself as a major sports league. It could not afford to alienate fans with boring games. The result was a number of rule changes designed to improve

The NBA's adoption of the shot clock was a result of Mikan's dominance.

the flow of the game, including the introduction of the twenty-four-second clock in 1954. This rule required teams to attempt a shot within twenty-four seconds after gaining possession of the ball. It favored teams that ran rather than those that set up plays more deliberately, as Minneapolis did for Mikan. It would result in increased scoring and a much faster paced, exciting game.

The Lakers' fall from the top lasted just one season. They took the crown again in 1951–52 by defeating the Knicks in a seven-game series. The season also marked another rule change brought about by the big man. The league widened the foul lane from six feet to twelve. Because a player could not remain in the lane for more than three seconds, Mikan was prevented from setting up as close to the hoop as possible. However, the rule did not drastically affect his performance. His scoring average did drop to 23.8 points per game, second in the league to Philadelphia's Paul Arizin. But on January 20, Mikan scored a career-high 61 points in a double-overtime contest against the Royals.

The Big Man Retires

The next year, Mikan led the NBA in rebounds and again finished second in scoring, although his averaged dropped to 20.6 points per game. The Lakers won yet another title. They compiled the best record in the league during the regular season, then defeated the Knicks in the finals of the playoffs for the second straight year.

Mikan was just twenty-nine years old when the 1953–54 season got underway, but his body felt much older. He always played hard and had the bumps and bruises to show for it. He broke at least ten bones during his career, and he was scheduled for surgery to have his left kneecap removed and replaced. Regardless, Mikan led the Lakers to a third straight championship that year—the sixth in seven seasons—as he finished fourth in the NBA in scoring (18.1 points per game) and second in rebounding (14.3 rebounds per game).

On September 25, 1954, Mikan shocked the basketball world by announcing his retirement. He had grown weary of the constant traveling that kept him away from his family. "I came home one day," he recalled, "and picked up my second son, Terry, and he began crying. He was afraid of me because he didn't know who I was. It broke my heart."[16] Mikan had also passed the bar two years earlier during the offseason and was eager to begin establishing a new career for himself. "I felt it was time to get started with the professional world outside of basketball,"[17] he said.

The Lakers offered Mikan a job as the team's general manager. He accepted the position and stayed for a year and a half. In the middle of the 1955–56 season, however, with the Lakers struggling to stay above .500, he left the sidelines and returned to the court. After a year's inactivity, he found it impossible to revert to his previous level of play. He averaged 10.5 points and 8.3 rebounds in thirty-seven games for Minneapolis, but it was not enough to keep the team from finishing with the first losing record in the franchise's history.

Mikan was one of basketball's first big men.

Mikan made a one-year attempt at coaching for the Lakers in 1957.

Keeping Active

Mikan took over as the Lakers' coach in 1957, but he stepped down the next January with the team's record at 9–30. After leaving the world of basketball, he practiced law, made an unsuccessful run for Congress, and worked as a stockbroker and travel agent.

In 1967 the NBA faced a challenge in the form of the new American Basketball Association (ABA). To gain credibility and recognition with fans, the owners of the new circuit hired Mikan as the league's first commissioner. One of his contributions was the innovative idea of using a multicolored basketball. Mikan said:

> We were trying to get the network television contract . . . and I thought the typical brown ball was very hard to see in a large auditorium. I decided on a ball with different-colored panels of red, white, and blue for three reasons. First, it was patriotic; second, the TV viewability was just fantastic; and

third, because of the salability of the ball. The young kids really liked it. [18]

Mikan resigned from his post in July 1969, in part because the league offices were to be moved to New York City. Mikan did not want to leave his home and law practice. He preferred to remain in "Siberia," his adopted state.

After being away from the game for a few years, Mikan's name was back in the news in the mid-1980s. He headed a task force whose goal was to bring NBA basketball back to Minneapolis. With the backing of local businessmen, he successfully lobbied the league to award Minnesota an expansion franchise—the Minnesota Timberwolves—for the 1989–90 season.

Mikan won every possible honor in his basketball career. He reached the top of his profession by a combination of talent, hard work, and determination. "George Mikan was the greatest competitor I've seen or been around in any sport," said teammate and former National Football League head coach Bud Grant. "He was amazing. He played hurt. He played when he'd had no sleep because of our travel schedule. And he always played at one speed—top." [19]

Mikan was a national scoring champion, NIT champion, three-time all-American, and National Player of the Year while in college. As a pro, he was a six-time scoring champ and five-time All-NBA First Team player, played in the first four NBA All-Star Games, and was named the All-Star Game MVP in 1953. Following his playing career, he was a coach, general manager, and league commissioner. His record made him a natural to be inducted into the Naismith Memorial Basketball Hall of Fame (named after James Naismith, the inventor of basketball) in 1959 as a member of the initial class of inductees. He was also named to the NBA 50th Anniversary All-Time Team in 1996, and he was voted the "Greatest Player in the First Half-Century" by the Associated Press.

Considering his career accomplishments, it is no wonder that he is referred to as "Mr. Basketball." His son Larry (also a former NBA player) says, "Dad is still a legend around [Minneapolis]." Larry's postscript, however, is undoubtedly what makes Mikan most proud. "And," he adds, "he's been a wonderful father to his six kids." [20]

CHAPTER 3

Elgin Baylor

Before superstars such as Julius Erving or Michael Jordan, Elgin Baylor entertained basketball fans everywhere with his acrobatic shots and gravity-defying moves. In an era when dunking was not fashionable and most players relied on the basic jump shot, Baylor played with a flair that was ahead of his time. "He's either got three hands or two basketballs," said former Knick Richie Guerin. "It's like guarding a flood."[21] Baylor was an innovative offensive force, and he is still considered by many to be the greatest forward ever.

The Early Years

John and Uzziel Baylor's third son was born on September 16, 1934. The proud new father took out his gold Elgin pocket watch to note the time. "And that's what he named me after,"[22] reported Elgin Baylor years later.

The Baylors lived in Washington, D.C., an area where racial discrimination was not uncommon. Because black children were not allowed to play in city playgrounds at the time, Baylor was not introduced to basketball until he was fourteen years old. When he did take up the sport, he quickly demonstrated an aptitude for it.

He tried out for the team at all-black Spingarn High School, and his talent was immediately apparent. As a senior, he made the All-Metropolitan team, an honor never before given to a black student. "He never shot much unless we needed points," said his coach, Dave Brown. "And even back then he was never excitable. In one big game, they got four quick fouls on him. I moved him outside and he made 44 points."[23]

At Spingarn, Baylor concentrated on sports more than he did on class work. (At one point, he dropped out of school and took a job working in a furniture store.) In addition to basketball, he played football, which attracted the attention of several colleges. Some were willing to end their racial restrictions to admit Baylor, but many shied away from him be-cause of his poor academic perfor-mance. He continued to play basketball, however, in the local recreational leagues.

After graduating from Spingarn, Baylor was offered a football schol-arship from the College of Idaho, when a friend who attended the school recommended him to the coach. Baylor never played football at Idaho, instead concentrating on basketball. In his only year at the school (1954–55), he averaged more than 31 points per game.

Following that season, the bas-ketball coach at Idaho was let go and Baylor transferred to Seattle University. The rules required that Baylor sit out a year after transfer-ring. To keep active, he played for an amateur team until he was al-lowed to suit up for the Chieftains in the fall of 1956.

When Baylor finally took to the court that year, he made an imme-diate impression. He led the nation

Elgin Baylor was selected first overall in the 1958 NBA draft.

in rebounding, averaging better than 20 boards per game. On offense, he averaged nearly 30 points a contest. The next year, he finished second in the nation in scoring (32.5 points per game) and third in rebounding (19.3 rebounds per game). Baylor was named first team all-American and led eighteenth-ranked Seattle to the postseason NCAA tournament. The Chieftains made it all the way to the championship game, but they lost to the University of Kentucky Wildcats, 84–72. Despite having a sub-par game in the final, (connecting on only 9 of 32 shots), Baylor was named the outstanding player of the tournament, having averaged 27 points for the five games.

The NBA Beckons

In the summer of 1958, Baylor was selected as the number-one overall pick in the NBA college draft by the financially troubled Lakers. The Lakers had struggled following the retirement of George Mikan in 1954, and they were looking for a gate attraction—a player who could bring fans out to the games.

Baylor still had a year of college eligibility remaining as a result of having sat out the year after he transferred. However, Lakers' owner Bob Short was able to sign him to a contract calling for a sizable annual salary of $20,000. The very day that Baylor signed, Short rejected an offer to sell the franchise because the offer fell well below his asking price of $250,000. (He would eventually sell it for more than $5 million seven years later.)

Baylor's signing saved the team. "If he had turned me down then," recalled Short, "I'd have been out of business. The club would have been bankrupt."[24] Instead, ticket sales increased and a renewed interest in the team was apparent. The Seattle all-American gave the team's fans hope for the future.

Like many young players, Baylor was apprehensive when he first joined the team. "When I went to training camp and saw all these big guys, I wondered if I really could make it," he later recalled. "But right after the first practice, I could sense that I was as good as they were."[25] In truth, he was much better.

Baylor's first year in the NBA (1958–59) was a rousing success. He made a name for himself with his rare combination of strength and grace. Baylor was not only able to score from the outside, but he was also a master at scoring in close to the basket. His inside

"The man with a thousand moves," seemed to defy gravity.

moves were often accompanied by a head twitch that was a kind of natural feint that misdirected opponents. When "the man with a thousand moves" finally went up for his shot, he seemed to defy gravity by hanging in the air longer than his opponent before putting the ball in the hoop.

Baylor averaged nearly 25 points per game that season for the fourth-highest mark in the league. He also finished third in rebounds and ninth in assists and ran away with Rookie of the Year honors. In that year's All-Star Game, Baylor scored 24 points and shared the game's MVP honors with Bob Pettit of the Hawks.

An incident that occurred in January gave an insight into the pride that drove Baylor. The Lakers had traveled to Charleston, West Virginia, for a game against the Cincinnati Royals. Baylor and two other black players on the team were denied access to a hotel where the club was staying. Rather than cause a fuss, Baylor simply decided that he would not play in the game. At first, some of the other players thought he was being selfish, hurting their

Baylor ran away with the Rookie of the Year honors in 1958–59.

chances of victory. When guard Rod Hundley asked him to reconsider, Baylor refused and explained why. "Rod," he said, "I'm a human being. I'm not an animal put in a cage and let out for show. They won't treat me like an animal."[26] The team lost that night, but Baylor had won the respect of everyone on the squad.

Feeling even more accepted by his teammates, Baylor's assured performance on the court translated into victories in the standings. The Lakers improved by fourteen games over their previous season's record, and they reached the finals in the playoffs where they were eventually beaten by the mighty Celtics. It was a significant improvement for Minneapolis, a team that had finished with the worst record in the league the year before.

On a personal level, Baylor's second season was even better than his first. His scoring average jumped to 29.6 points per game. On November 8, 1959, he set an NBA record by scoring 64 points in a single contest, breaking the old mark of 63 set by Joe Fulks of the Philadelphia Warriors in 1949. Breaking that record was especially sweet because it came against the rival Celtics.

The Lakers, however, struggled all year. Baylor's college coach, John Castellani, had been hired as head coach. He was replaced when the team started out with just 11 wins in its first thirty-six games. Former Lakers star Jim Pollard took over the club, but he fared no better. The team finished with a record of 25–50 and attendance continued to fall. Minneapolis fans were not eager to pay to see a losing team, even one with Baylor as its star. Following the season, owner Short moved the team to Los Angeles in hopes of rejuvenating the franchise.

Coming Up Short

The club's prospects improved when it drafted Jerry West with the second pick in the 1960 draft. With West now drawing much of the opposition's attention with his deadly jump shots from outside, Baylor flourished. He averaged nearly 35 points per game, while taking down a career-high 1,447 rebounds for the season. On November 15, he scored an unprecedented record 71 points against the Knicks, setting a new NBA single-game standard. "Elgin did nothing unusual in that game," recalled former Knick Johnny Green. "It was just a typical Baylor performance. He just came down the floor, his teammates would clear out an area, and he'd shoot a jump shot or a driving layup, followed up by a rebound if he missed. Each particular shot had nothing amazing about it. It was just that Elgin was such an amazing player." [27]

Although the Lakers again finished with a record below .500, they advanced to the Western Division Finals in the playoffs. There they faced the Hawks for the third consecutive year. The Lakers lost

November 15, 1960, Baylor scored an unprecedented 71 points.

to the Hawks in a thrilling seven-game series in which their last three losses were by a total of just four points.

In 1961, outside the world of basketball, the Cold War heated up between the United States and the Soviet Union. In the wake of the Berlin crisis, Baylor was called away to active military duty. He was stationed at Fort Lewis, Washington, and although he was available to play only on weekends for a good portion of the year, Elgin made the most of his time on the court. He averaged a career-high 38.3 points per contest for the forty-eight games in which he appeared.

Despite playing under this handicap, the Lakers dominated the Western Division. The combination of West and Baylor accounted for nearly 70 points every time they took to the floor together. Unfortunately, it was not enough to get past the Celtics, whom they faced in the NBA Finals.

Despite the loss of Baylor due to military service, the Lakers dominated the Western Division.

Baylor again was sensational, scoring a playoff-record 61 points in a Game 5 win to put them ahead three games to two. He was successful on 22 of 46 field-goal attempts and 17 of 19 free throws to break the record of 56 points that Philadelphia Warriors center Wilt Chamberlain had set just weeks before. Baylor's mark would stand for twenty-four years, until Michael Jordan scored 63 points in a 1986 first-round contest against the Celtics. Baylor's performance was all the more remarkable because he was being guarded by Boston's Tom Sanders, one of the top defensive forwards of the day. "Elgin was just a machine in that game,"[28] recalled Sanders. In addition to his 61 points, Baylor also pulled down 22 rebounds in the game as the Lakers won, 126–121. Years later he would modestly say, "All I remember is that we won the game." [29] (Four decades later, his mark still stands as a finals series record.)

The Celtics, however, bounced back to take the last two contests. The seventh—and final—game of the series ranks as a classic. With time running out on the clock, Lakers' guard Frank Selvy took a jump shot that would have given Los Angeles the title. Instead, the ball rolled off the rim and the game went into overtime. Boston outscored the Lakers in the extra stanza to win their fourth straight NBA championship. Unbeknownst to Baylor, it would be the closest he would come to winning a championship ring. He averaged an incredible 38.6 points for the thirteen postseason games.

Beset by Injuries

During the next four years the Lakers compiled one of the most frustrating streaks imaginable. They met the Celtics in the championship series three more times. Each time, the Celtics prevailed.

Back from the service in time for the 1962–63 season, Baylor put together one of his greatest seasons. He finished second in the league behind Wilt Chamberlain in scoring (34.0 points per game), third in free-throw percentage (.837), fifth in rebounds (14.3 rebounds per game), and fifth in assists (4.8 assists per game). These accomplishments made him the first player in NBA history to finish in the top five in four major categories.

In 1964–65, in the first game of the Western Division Finals against the Baltimore Bullets, Baylor suffered a devastating injury. He went up for a jump shot and came down in agony. As he later recalled, "Something pulled. I didn't know what it was. I forgot about the ball as soon as I felt it. But I could run. I went up and down the court a few times, but it hurt so much and I didn't know what it was, so I decided I better get out." [30] How he was able to run even a single step is hard to understand. The top part of his left patella had somehow broken off from the rest of the kneecap. He was operated on the very next day, but prospects for his future were dim.

Baylor spent the summer unsure if he would ever play again. "I'd never broken anything before," he said, "so at first I just didn't know what to think, whether to be scared or what. . . . Finally, I just accepted the fact that I would never play again. I just worried about being a normal person—could I fish or play golf, just move around ever again? I thought that way. And then . . . it all got better."[31]

Amazingly, Baylor recovered in time to play in the 1965-66 season, but his effectiveness was significantly curtailed. He overcompensated for the knee, and the result was extra stress placed

Baylor lays the ball up after returning from a severe knee injury.

on his right leg. Baylor was out for a month and came back more unsure of himself than ever. As Lakers' announcer Chick Hearn put it, "It was like watching Citation [a thoroughbred horse who won racing's Triple Crown in 1948] run on spavined legs [a condition in horses characterized by swelling of the joints].[32]

As the playoffs approached, Baylor's doctor—the renowned sports orthopedic surgeon Robert Kerlan—told him the time for caution was past. "I told him that he either had to go out and test it and find out," said Kerlan, "or otherwise he might as well come over and rest with me."[33]

Baylor followed his doctor's recommendation and the results were impressive. He averaged more than 25 points and 14 rebounds a game over the last month of the regular season, and scored 41 points in Game 5 of the finals series against Boston. Overall, he averaged 16.6 points per game for the year, the first time his average had dropped below 20. "It was an amazing recovery, certainly," said Kerlan, "but only if you consider it simply overcoming an injury. The man is often the most important thing, and in view of the sort of man Elgin is, then, maybe, we should have even expected it."[34]

Baylor bounced back to average almost 25 points per game for another four years. The Lakers, however, continued to fall short in their bid for a championship. They reached the finals in both 1969 and 1970, but lost in seven-game series both years.

At the beginning of the 1970–71 season, Baylor tore his Achilles tendon and saw action in just two games all year. He tried to come back the next fall, but was forced to retire nine games into the season. "I've always wanted to perform on the court up to the level and up to the standards I have established throughout my career," he said. "I do not want to prolong my career to the time when I can't maintain those standards."[35]

The very next day, the Lakers defeated the Bullets, 110–106, to begin a record-setting thirty-three game winning streak. Ironically, Los Angeles captured the championship that season, while Baylor ended his playing career without ever winning the coveted championship.

The End of the Line

At the time of his retirement, Baylor was the third-highest scorer in NBA history. Today, three decades later, his career scoring av-

Baylor poses with his Basketball Hall of Fame trophy.

erage of 27.4 points per game has been topped by just two men—Wilt Chamberlain and Michael Jordan. Baylor averaged more than 30 points a game three times, and made the All-NBA First Team in ten of his first eleven seasons. With his retirement, the Lakers not only lost a great player on the court, but they also lost a leader in the locker room. Baylor was admired and re-spected by all his teammates, and was known for giving advice and resolving conflicts.

Three years after hanging up his sneakers, Baylor was offered a job as assistant coach with the expansion New Orleans Jazz in their maiden season. He accepted and remained in the position for two years. In December 1976 he was promoted to head coach, replacing Bill van Breda Kolff twenty-six games into the season. In two and a half years with Baylor in charge, the Jazz compiled a record of 86–135. It was during this period that he received sport's highest honor: induction into the Naismith Memorial Basketball Hall of Fame.

Baylor eventually moved on to the Los Angeles Clippers, where he has been the executive vice president of basketball operations since 1986. In 1996, a quarter century after he played his last game, another honor was bestowed upon him. He was named to the NBA 50th Anniversary All-Time Team. It was a fitting tribute for the man whom, according to *Sports Illustrated*, the word "superstar" was invented and first applied to. As former teammate Tommy Hawkins once stated, "pound for pound, no one was ever as great as Elgin Baylor." [36]

CHAPTER 4

Jerry West

One of Jerry West's nicknames—"Mr. Clutch"—sums him up. He was the man his teammates looked to when the game was on the line, the player who could handle the pressure when one shot could decide the outcome. One of the greatest pure shooters in the history of the game, West was able to put the ball in the basket from anywhere on the court. In addition to being a high scorer, he was also one of the top defensive players of his day and an intense competitor.

Coal-Mining Country

One of the most famous nicknames in pro basketball annals is "Zeke from Cabin Creek," bestowed on Jerry West by his Los Angeles Lakers' teammate, Elgin Baylor. The name, unfortunately, is not entirely accurate. Jerry Alan West was not from Cabin Creek, West Virginia, but rather from nearby Cheylan, where he was born on May 28, 1938; Cabin Creek was the location of the local post office. His father was a poor coal-mine electrician who struggled to provide the necessities of life for his family, which included his wife and five children.

Jerry—the fourth child—was shy and introspective as a youngster, in large part because of a family tragedy that occurred when

49

Jerry West lays the ball up against the Knicks.

he was twelve years old. His older brother David, who was serving in the armed forces, was killed in the Korean War. The young Jerry adored his brother, and the death deeply affected him. "He was almost a perfect person," said West. "You would almost say to yourself, 'My goodness, why didn't it happen to me?' because this person was so good. . . . It changed me from being extremely aggressive to unbelievably passive, and maybe more introverted than I should have been at that point in my life."[37]

Jerry began to keep to himself more and more. He spent countless hours shooting baskets at a hoop that was nailed to a shed outside a neighbor's house. He practiced on the dirt-covered court in all kinds of weather, even wearing gloves if the weather required them. In time, Jerry's obsession began to worry his mother. He would skip meals and practice shooting until his fingers bled. He became so thin and malnourished that he required vitamin injections.

West's dedication was also stoked by his failure to make his junior high school team. His constant practice eventually paid off, however, and he made the varsity team at East Bank High School as a junior. He played sporadically that year, but over the summer he shot up six inches in height. As a six-foot-tall senior, he blossomed on the court. He averaged more than 32 points per game for East Bank, in the process becoming the first high school player in the state's history to score 900 points in a season: His shooting and all-around play led the school to the 1956 state championship. In his honor, fans renamed the town West Bank for a day. On March 24 of every year since (the anniversary of the championship game), East Bank High School changes its name to West Bank.

A Mountaineer Legend

By the time West graduated, word of his talent had reached audiences far from home. He was truly a local hero, courted by more than sixty colleges. He finally chose West Virginia University because he had followed the Mountaineers on radio ever since he was a young boy, and he dreamed of playing for them some day. His choice disappointed recruiters from dozens of other schools.

West certainly did not disappoint Mountaineer fans. He won all-American honors twice while averaging nearly 25 points per game for

Courted by more than sixty colleges, West finally decided on West Virginia.

his college career. In one memorable game against the University of Kentucky when he was a senior, he broke his nose during the first half of play. Barely able to breathe, he returned to the lineup for the second half with his nose stuffed with gauze. He proceeded to score 19 more points to help West Virginia to an upset win over the nationally ranked Wildcats.

In 1959 West guided the Mountaineers all the way to the championship game of the NCAA tournament. There, West Virginia lost to the University of California by a score of 71–70, despite his scoring 28 points. He led his team in scoring and rebounding in every one of the five postseason contests, and he tied a tournament record with his 160 points. This did little to console him, however. He took absolutely no pleasure if his team did not win. As former Laker teammate and head coach Pat Riley would later say, "He hated losing more than any man I've ever been around in my life."[38]

By this time, West's reputation as a high-stakes scorer and as an intense competitor had spread across the country. It was generally agreed among basketball observers that he and the University of Cincinnati's Oscar Robertson were the top two seniors eligible for the NBA draft that year, although West had his reservations about his future. "I didn't think I was good enough to play in the NBA," he admitted.[39]

The Lakers did not share his doubts. With Robertson headed to the Royals as a territorial choice (where a team could select a local player to help build a fan base), West was available to be taken with the first overall pick. They selected him to team up with their other superstar, Elgin Baylor.

At first, West was disappointed. He had been hoping to be drafted by the Knicks, who had the second pick. His disappointment disappeared, however, when it was announced that the Lakers were moving to Los Angeles. He signed for $15,000, but before he could don the blue and white of the Lakers, he traveled to Rome to play for the U.S. team in the 1960 summer Olympics. Considered by many to be the greatest Olympic team ever assembled (of those limited to amateur players), the squad consisted of ten players who continued their careers in the NBA. The Americans ran over the competition, winning each of their eight games by at least 24 points, by an average of 42 points. West returned to the States with a gold medal.

In the 1960 summer Olympics in Rome, Jerry West represented the U.S.

"Unbelievable Frustration"

With the Lakers coming off a 25–50 record the previous season, owner Bob Short hired Fred Schaus, West's coach at West Virginia, as the team's new head coach. From their time together in Morgantown, Schaus viewed West as the perfect guard. "He is the man that has everything," he said. "A fine shooting touch, speed, quickness, all the physical assets, including a tremendous dedication to the game."[40]

West needed some time to adjust to the pros and to his new teammates. "It was the worst year of my life in basketball,"[41] he would later say. By the second half of the season, however, he and Baylor were on their way to becoming the most lethal one-two punch in the league. West averaged 17.6 points a game as a rookie while Baylor contributed 34.8. Together, they led the club to a second-place finish in the Western Division of the NBA. In the playoffs, they extended the heavily-favored Hawks to seven games before losing to them in the Western Division Finals. The Hawks won the last two contests by a total of three points.

Because Baylor missed a good part of the 1961–62 season to military service, West took on a larger share of the offensive load. He raised his average more than 13 points to 30.8 per game. On January 17 of that season, he poured through 63 points in a game against the Knicks. At the time, it was the most points ever scored in a single game by a guard. West increased his average to 31.5 in the playoffs. It was not enough, however, to get Los Angeles past the mighty Celtics in the NBA Finals.

In Game 3, with the series tied at one game apiece, West gave one of his typically solid performances. He sank two jump shots within the last minute to tie the game. With just three seconds left in regulation time, he intercepted a pass from Boston's Sam Jones and scored on a layup to give Los Angeles a 117–115 victory. "I've never forgotten it," said West. "Everyone wants to hit a home run in the ninth inning to win a big game. That was my home run."[42]

Despite numerous injuries in the 1961–62 season, West recorded the most points in a game by a guard.

After a loss in Game 4, the Lakers won Game 5 to go ahead, three games to two. Boston came back to even the series in Game 6, setting the stage for a dramatic Game 7 that would become an excruciating loss for West. With the score tied at 100–100, Lakers guard Frank Selvy put up a fifteen-foot jump shot that would have given his team the title had it gone in. Instead, the ball bounced off the rim as time ran out. In the five-minute overtime, the Celtics would not be denied. They outscored Los Angeles, 10 points to 7, to gain the victory and their fourth consecutive title. The loss to the Celtics was a scenario that would be repeated several times in the years to come. It would be, as West described it, a source of "unbelievable frustration."[43]

In 1962–63, West suffered a leg injury and was forced to sit out twenty-seven games. He returned to help the club to another Western Division title, but the Celtics again blocked the team's path to the championship. This time Boston defeated Los Angeles in six games, winning four times by an average of just 4 points.

Following a sub-par season the next year, the Lakers bounced back in 1964–65. Unfortunately, Baylor blew out his knee just five minutes into Game 1 of the Western Division Finals against the Bullets. West took over and proceeded to score 49 points in the Lakers' 121–115 victory. The next game saw him score 52 in another Los Angeles win. The Bullets evened the series with wins in the next two games, despite 44 and 48 points from West. He followed up with games of 43 and 42 points as the Lakers won to advance to the finals. West's six-game average of 46.3 points is a playoff series record that has never been topped. So, too, is his string of six games with 40 or more points.

Without Baylor to take pressure off West, the Lakers were easy prey for the Celtics in the NBA Finals. Boston won in five games, despite nearly 34 points per game from the superlative guard. West's average for the eleven playoff contests was an incredible 40.6 points per game.

Boston dashed Los Angeles' title hopes again in 1965–66. The seventh game of the series was a two-point victory for Boston and another frustrating loss for West. The Celtics won again in six games in 1967–68, and in seven the following season, the final one by another 2-point margin. That year, West became the only player from a losing team to win the finals MVP award.

An intense West sits on the bench minutes prior to scoring the game-tying
shot against the Knicks.

The Celtics failed to make the playoffs in 1969–70. The Lakers
fought past the Phoenix Suns in seven games, then swept the Atlanta Hawks (relocated from St. Louis) in four straight to meet the
Knicks for the NBA crown. The teams split the first two games,
providing the setting in Game 3 for one of the most famous shots
in NBA history.

With the score tied at 100–100 in New York's Madison Square
Garden, Knick forward Dave DeBusschere's jump shot with three
seconds left in the game appeared to seal the Lakers' fate. West,
however, had not given up. He took the inbounds pass from Wilt
Chamberlain, aimed, and let it fly from about sixty feet away. The
ball sailed through the hoop to tie the score as the final buzzer
sounded. (Had the game been played today, with the modern
three-point shot in effect, it would have given the Lakers the win.)
New York guard Walt Frazier remembered the shot vividly. "The
man's crazy," he recalled thinking. "He looks determined. He
thinks it's really going in!"[44]

Unfortunately, the Lakers could not contain the Knicks in the
five-minute overtime; they lost 111–108. West finished with 34
points and 9 assists. He could not bear to talk about his miracu-

lous shot, however. "It doesn't really matter, does it," he said, "because we lost."[45] When the Knicks went on to win the seven-game series, it was another disappointment added to West's list.

A Championship at Last

Prior to the start of the 1971–72 season, West seriously considered retirement. Assorted injuries and broken bones had taken a toll on his thirty-three-year-old body. (His nose had been broken at least eight times.) After having come so close, so often, however, he could not bear to walk away without a championship.

Former Celtic Bill Sharman took over as the Lakers' coach in the fall of 1971, and helped West reach his goal. Although Baylor was forced to retire because of leg injuries, West was still surrounded with solid players, and the Lakers put together a season to be remembered. West averaged nearly 26 points per game and led the league in assists. Los Angeles rolled to a 69–13 mark and set a new NBA record for victories in a season. Along the way, they established another record by winning an impressive thirty-three consecutive games.

In the playoffs, the Lakers ran over the Bulls, the defending champion Milwaukee Bucks, and the Knicks to finally get West his coveted championship ring. His twelve-year quest had at long last resulted in success. Ironically, however, West did not enjoy the moment as much as he thought he would. "You've heard that song, 'Is That All There Is?'" he said. "That's pretty much how I felt. It still never, even to this day, will replace the pain of those other losses."[46]

West finally achieved his coveted championship after a long twelve-year quest.

West played one more season for the Lakers, then retired as the third-highest scorer in the league's history. He realized that injuries had reduced his effectiveness. "I could still play," he said, "but I couldn't play the way I wanted to play. That's the difference."[47]

Upon retiring, West was a ten-time first-team NBA all-star, and he was the only player in history to be named to play in every All-Star Game in each season of his career. He also was named to the NBA All-Defensive Team four times in the first five times teams were chosen. His ability to make clutch baskets was legendary. "He was undoubtedly the greatest shooter when the game was on the line," said Bill Sharman. "Throughout his career, he must have won forty to fifty games with the last basket."[48] West's status as one of the game's all-time greats was made official in 1979 when he was elected to the Naismith Memorial Basketball Hall of Fame.

West retired in 1972–73, but not before recording his name as one of the greatest to ever play.

*As a front office executive, West (left) was instrumental in building the
Laker franchise of today.*

Into the Front Office

After being away from the game for two years, West was hired by
the Lakers prior to the 1976–77 season to replace Bill Sharman as
coach. He spent three years in that position, compiling a record of
145–101. The Lakers made the playoffs each of those seasons and
were eliminated by the eventual NBA champion two times.

When Jerry Buss purchased the team from Jack Kent Cooke after the end of the 1978–79 season, he brought in Jack McKinney as
his new coach. West became a special consultant to the team, a position he held for another three years. Just before the 1982–83 season, he was promoted to general manager of the team, and took
charge of the day-to-day operations of the club. To the list of positions he held with the club, he added the title executive vice president of basketball operations in 1995.

As a front office executive, West helped to build the great Lakers' teams of the 1980s. His acquisitions included Byron Scott,

A.C. Green, Sam Perkins, and Vlade Divac. After Laker fortunes had dropped following the retirements of Kareem Abdul-Jabbar, Magic Johnson, and James Worthy, it was West who gambled by trading away several players so the team would have the opportunity to lure Shaquille O'Neal away from the Orlando Magic.

As a judge of talent, West had no peers. It was he who lauded high school student Kobe Bryant on the eve of the 1996 draft saying, "I've just seen the best workout by a teenager, ever."[49] Bryant, of course, has gone on to become one of the most talented players in the league.

West's accomplishments may sometimes have been overlooked by the public, but never by his peers. "I voted him Executive of the Year every year he was there,"[50] recalled Indiana Pacers' president Donnie Walsh. He was there long enough as general manager to add six NBA titles to go with the one he won as a player. Those accomplishments were accompanied by a tremendous amount of self-induced stress through his constant striving for perfection. "The average person wouldn't understand the pressure and stress that I've felt in my life," he said shortly after announcing his retirement in August 2000. "I need to get off this merry-go-round for a while."[51] He also acknowledged his desire to spend more time with his family. "I have a relatively young family," he said. "I think you need a father in the house, and that's the most important thing in my life right now."[52]

West's success was perhaps best summed up by former adversary Bill Russell of the Celtics. "The greatest honor a man can have" said Russell on Jerry West Night at the Great Western Forum in 1971, "is the respect and friendship of his peers. You have that more than any man I know."[53] The league itself has honored West by using a silhouette of him driving to the hoop on the official NBA logo.

CHAPTER 5

Kareem Abdul-Jabbar

K areem Abdul-Jabbar is professional basketball's all-time lead-ing scorer, and arguably the greatest all-around big man ever to play the game. He dominated the sport at every level, from high school through the pros, playing with a grace and agility never before seen in a man his size. A six-time MVP, he ruled over the NBA for twenty seasons. For former Lakers' coach Pat Riley, there is no question as to Abdul-Jabbar's place among the greats of the game. "Why judge anymore?" said Riley. "When a man has broken records, won championships, endured tremendous criti-cism and responsibility, why judge? Let's toast him as the greatest player ever."[54]

A Local Hero

When Ferdinand Lewis Alcindor Jr. was born on April 16, 1947, he weighed a hefty thirteen pounds and measured nearly twenty-two inches. No one was shocked at Lew's size, however, because both his parents were above average in height. His father was a six-foot, two-inch tall lieutenant with the New York City Transit Authority police; his wife, Cora, stood six-foot one. Alcindor was a strict dis-ciplinarian and his wife was overprotective of their only child.

The Alcindors lived in the Inwood section of upper Manhattan where Lew attended St. Jude's elementary school. The youngster loved to swim, ice skate, and play baseball, winning his first medals and trophies in those sports. One of his dreams was to become a pitcher for the Brooklyn Dodgers. As he grew older, he became more self-conscious of his above-average size. He gravitated toward basketball, where his height was a distinct advantage. By the eighth grade, his talents were obvious to everyone who saw him play. Prep schools from the area began vying for his attention as he grew to prominence in local basketball circles. He eventually chose Power Memorial Academy, an all-boys Catholic school on the city's West Side.

Lew Alcindor tips the ball into the basket for Power Memorial Academy.

Standing six-foot, eight-inches tall, Lew made coach Jack Donohue's varsity basketball team as a freshman. With Donohue's help and a rigid training schedule, Lew began to hone his game, smoothing off the rough edges and losing much of his adolescent awkwardness. His positive attitude played a big part in his progress. "Most big boys are awkward," said Donohue. "But after his freshman year, you couldn't say that about Lewie any more. Sure, he was given talent. But others have had that and didn't develop it. I think Lewie's biggest asset was tremendous pride."[55]

His basketball career at Power was an unqualified success. The team went 27–0 in Lew's sophomore season and won the New York City Catholic High School basketball championship as he topped the squad in scoring and rebounding. They repeated the next year, winning all twenty-five of their games. In the 1963–64 season (Lew's senior year), the club won its first nineteen games, extending its consecutive-game winning streak to seventy-one, before being upset by Maryland's De-Matha High School. It was Power's only loss as it won its third straight NYC Catholic High School championship. DeMatha's defense limited Lew to 16 points, and he blamed himself for the loss. Coach Donohue, however, put things in perspective. "You played the way you always have," he said. "If you want the blame for this one, you'll have to take credit for the other seventy-one."[56]

Lew scored a city-record 2,067 points in his career at Power on his way to becoming the most publicized prep player in the country. When it came time to pick a college, the seven-foot tall Lew had his choice of more than one hundred schools that offered him scholarships. Former United Nations undersecretary Ralph Bunche recommended that Lew choose the University of California at Los Angeles (UCLA), where Bunche had received his degree. Lew Alcindor was impressed with the school's athletic and academic programs, and enrolled there in the fall of 1965.

National Championships

Alcindor's first basketball game for the UCLA Bruins was a rousing success. He scored 31 points to lead the freshman team to a 75–60 win over the varsity, even though the varsity was the two-time defending national champion and ranked number one in the preseason basketball polls. The "Brubabes" went undefeated that season, as Alcindor set freshman records for points scored and rebounds, as well as a new single-game scoring mark.

When Alcindor stepped up to varsity as a sophomore in 1966–67, he joined a team that was used to success. UCLA had won the national championship in two of the three previous seasons and had a solid core of returning players. There was no question, however, that Alcindor's talents overshadowed those of the others. "No matter how good many of the Bruins are," wrote Frank Deford in *Sports Illustrated*, "and how well they are coached by John Wooden, their game is Lew Alcindor. . . . Alcindor's influence is so pervasive that it is difficult to determine how good his teammates really are."[57]

Alcindor tosses a hook, leading UCLA to an 88-2 record in three years.

The combination proved impossible to beat. Alcindor scored a school-record 56 points against the University of Southern California (USC) in his first-ever varsity contest, leading USC coach Vic Bubas to say, "He destroys you, that's what he does."[58] Alcindor broke that record in February, when he scored 61 points against Washington State University, a team foolish enough to play a straight man-to-man defense. (Most schools played zone defense where two or three men would converge on Alcindor when he got the ball. In a man-to-man, each defensive player was responsible for only one offensive man, and no one man could stop Alcindor by himself.)

For the year, Alcindor averaged nearly 30 points and 15 rebounds per game. UCLA went undefeated and won another national title, the first of three they would win with him at center.
Opposing coaches tried different strategies to stop Alcindor, but
nothing worked. As Notre Dame's coach Johnny Dee said, "The
only way to beat Alcindor is to hope for the three Fs: Foreign
court, friendly officials, and foul out Alcindor."[59]

The NCAA also tried to limit his effectiveness. It banned the
dunk shot following his sophomore year in an effort to check his
dominance. The move proved futile, however. In Alcindor's three
years, UCLA compiled an amazing 88–2 record. He was a three-
time first team all-American, a two-time National Player of the Year,
and the first three-time NCAA Tournament Most Outstanding
Player. At the time of his graduation, he was the leading scorer in
UCLA history and the sixth-highest
scorer in major college annals. Professional basketball loomed as his
next world to conquer.

Next Stop, the Pros

Upon his graduation in 1969, Alcindor was drafted by both the
Milwaukee Bucks of the NBA and
the New Jersey Nets of a new
league that had begun play in
1967–68, the American Basketball
Association (ABA). To avoid a bid-
ding war, Alcindor asked the two
teams to submit sealed bids. Milwaukee's contract offer of more
than $1 million was the higher of
the two. Despite the Nets' insistence that they would surpass that
amount, Alcindor kept his word
and signed with the Bucks.

As an expansion team the previous season, the Bucks had compiled
a record of just 27–55. Alcindor—
now almost seven-foot, two-inches

*After graduating from UCLA,
Alcindor signed with the
Milwaukee Bucks.*

tall—immediately transformed them into winners, powering the Bucks to a 56–26 mark and second-place finish in the Eastern Division. He averaged 28.8 points and 14.5 rebounds per game, finishing second and third in the league, respectively, in those categories. Alcindor won Rookie of the Year honors and established himself as a major force in the league.

During the offseason, the Bucks acquired all-star guard Oscar Robertson from the Cincinnati Royals. Robertson combined with Alcindor to take Milwaukee to the top of the NBA standings in 1970–71. The Bucks led the league with 66 victories, including one streak of 20 in a row. They raced through the playoffs to the final series, where they swept the Baltimore Bullets to take the league championship. Alcindor won the scoring title and his first MVP award. He capped his season by also being named MVP of the finals.

In the following offseason, Alcindor reached an important personal decision. Over the years, he had become acutely aware of social injustice and racial discrimination in America. As a writer in *Newsweek* wrote in 1967, "The more he reads . . . and the more he sees of life off the basketball floor, the more Alcindor burns with resentment and racial pride."[60] He had embraced the Islamic faith while in college, and he made it known in 1968 when he joined the black athletes' Olympic boycott. He said then that he did not want to compete for a country that he felt was "abusing my people."[61] Then, in 1971, he went public with his Moslem name—Kareem Abdul-Jabbar—which means "noble, powerful servant." Many fans were outraged, particularly among white America. He received a great deal of unfavorable publicity, which caused Abdul-Jabbar to become moody and unapproachable.

The bad press did not affect his performance, however. Over the succeeding years, Abdul-Jabbar enhanced his reputation as a powerful warrior in the NBA. He won two more MVP awards with Milwaukee, and made one more appearance in the finals series in 1974. The Bucks played the Celtics that year in an exciting seven-game series. With Boston leading three games to two, Milwaukee was in a do-or-die situation in Game 6. The contest went into double overtime before Abdul-Jabbar won it with one of his trademark skyhooks (an impossible-to-block hook shot), as his signature shot had been christened by the Bucks' play-by-play broadcaster, Eddie Doucette. Unfortunately, the Celtics bounced back to take Game 7 and capture the championship.

After the 1974 season, Oscar Robertson retired. The Bucks' streak of four successive division titles ended and the team dropped into last place with a 38–44 record. Discouraged and unhappy, Abdul-Jabbar requested a trade to either New York or Los Angeles, cities that he felt would better suit his needs with their large African-American communities and cultural advantages. The Bucks accommodated him, sending him to the Lakers in exchange for four players: Junior Bridgeman, Dave Meyers, Elmore Smith, and Brian Winters. He returned to the city of his college triumphs, ready to lead the Lakers to glory.

Abdul-Jabbar sets up for his trademark hook shot in the 1974 playoffs.

Beginning of a Dynasty

Since Wilt Chamberlain's retirement two years before, the Lakers' fortunes had been on the decline. In 1974–75, the team had finished in last place with a record of 30–52. In his first year on the West Coast, Abdul-Jabbar led the league in rebounding and blocked shots. He won his fourth MVP award, but the Lakers still finished out of the playoffs with a 40–42 mark.

The next year, Abdul-Jabbar sparked the club to a ten-game improvement as he won his fifth MVP award for his all-around play in only his eighth season in the league. He won again the following year as the Lakers—under new coach Jerry West—returned to the top spot in the Pacific Division with a mark of 53–29. In the playoffs, they lost in the Western Conference Finals to the eventual champions, the Portland Trail Blazers.

The 1978 season proved a frustrating one for Abdul-Jabbar and the Lakers.

The 1977–78 season was a disappointing one for both Abdul-Jabbar and the Lakers. The year began on a negative note two minutes into the very first game. Abdul-Jabbar believed he had been elbowed by Milwaukee center Kent Benson. Uncharacteristically, Abdul-Jabbar threw a punch at Benson, breaking his own hand and sidelining him for the first two months of the season. He was also fined $5,000 by the league for his actions. Later that year, Los Angeles forward Kermit Washington delivered a punch that shattered the face of Houston Rockets forward Rudy Tomjanovich. Tomjanovich required reconstructive surgery, and Washington was fined and suspended for sixty days. Despite these two losses, the Lakers managed to qualify for the playoffs, but they were defeated by the Seattle SuperSonics, a combination they repeated the following year.

The Missing Piece

Although Abdul-Jabbar continued to post numbers worthy of the premiere center in the league, the Lakers did not meet expectations. When they drafted Magic Johnson from Michigan State with the first pick in the 1979 draft, however, the final piece of the puzzle was added. Just as Oscar Robertson blended in with Abdul-Jabbar when he joined Milwaukee, so, too, did Johnson complement Abdul-Jabbar in Los Angeles.

The dynamic duo led the Lakers to a 60-win season en route to the NBA Championship in 1979–80. At age thirty-three, Kareem was still able to dominate play at an age when many players are struggling to stay in the league. "I know the game a lot better," said Abdul-Jabbar. "I'm physically stronger . . . and I'm still quicker than most centers in the league."[62]

Abdul-Jabbar severely sprained his ankle in Game 5 of the finals, but he still managed to score 40 points in the Lakers' 108–103 win. The next day, with Abdul-Jabbar out of action, Johnson stepped up to score 42 points to lead Los Angeles to victory in the final game. "We know you're hurting, big fella," said Johnson to his teammate after the game, "but we want you to get up and do some dancing tonight!"[63] For the year, Abdul-Jabbar won a record sixth MVP award, while Johnson was named MVP of the NBA Finals.

The Lakers would win four more NBA titles over the next decade, taking nine division crowns in the final ten years of Abdul-Jabbar's career. He continued to average better than 20 points a game into his late thirties, defying the ravages of time. As he

At age 33, Abdul-Jabbar still dominated the game of basketball.

grew older, he concentrated more on keeping himself fit. He practiced yoga and the martial arts, and he remained trim and muscular. Abdul-Jabbar's relationship with the fans also improved with time, as he became more accessible to the media.

Kareem continued to display the talents and determination that had characterized his play through the first half of his career. His signature skyhook had become perhaps the best-known, most effective, and unstoppable weapon of its day. It was with this shot that he scored career point number 31,420 on April 5, 1984, to move past Wilt Chamberlain as the league's all-time leading scorer.

Perhaps the most satisfying championship of the six won by Abdul-Jabbar was Los Angeles' victory over the Celtics in 1985. In Game 1, Kareem was held to just 12 points and 3 rebounds by Boston's Robert Parish. Many observers felt it was time for the thirty-eight-year-old superstar to hang up his sneakers.

Abdul-Jabbar, however, was determined to prove them wrong. Over the next two days, he dedicated himself completely to preparing for the remainder of the series. The preparation consisted of hours of watching game films and lengthy practice sessions that included countless wind sprints. He exhorted his teammates to rise to the occasion. "We may not win," he told them, "but let's make it worthy of us."[64]

The Lakers proceeded to win four of the next five games, securing another NBA crown. In the four Los Angeles victories Abdul-Jabbar averaged 30.2 points, 11.3 rebounds, 6.5 assists, and 2.0 blocked shots per game. It was a sparkling performance by a remarkable player. As coach Pat Riley told reporters, "What you saw was passion."[65] For his efforts, Kareem won the NBA Finals MVP award for the second time—fourteen years after having won it while with the Bucks. "He defies logic," said Riley. "He's the most unique and durable athlete of our time, the best you'll ever see. You'd better enjoy him while he's here."[66]

Life After the NBA

The 1986–87 season—when Kareem was forty years old—was the first in which his scoring average dropped below 20 points per game. He played two more years for Los Angeles, retiring after his twentieth season. He was honored by fans and players alike at every arena in the league during his final appearances in the

Abdul-Jabbar hoists his Finals MVP trophy after defeating the Boston Celtics in 1985.

1988–89 season. As he told a reporter several years after he retired, "The '80s made up for all the abuse I took during the '70s. I outlived all my critics. By the time I retired, everybody saw me as a venerable institution. Things do change."[67]

Since retiring, Abdul-Jabbar has been involved in many causes, devoting much of his time and energy to battling hunger and illiteracy. He has also done extensive research on the history of oppressed peoples. In 1995 he traveled to the Fort Apache Indian Reservation in Whiteriver, Arizona, to research the Buffalo Soldiers, an African-American cavalry that served on the Old West frontier. The material eventually became part of his book, *Black Profiles in Courage: A Legacy in African-American Achievement.*

While at Whiteriver, he took a job as the assistant coach of the basketball team at Alchesay High School on the reservation to gain experience that might someday lead to a college or professional position. "I know the game inside and out from playing it at the highest levels for 25 years," said Abdul-Jabbar. "What I am learning here is how to communicate what I know, but also to develop the altogether different talent of reaching inside other people to pull out their best effort."[68] He recounted his experiences at Whiteriver in his 2000 book *A Season on the Reservation: My Sojourn with the White Mountain Apache.*

In February 2000, Abdul-Jabbar returned to the NBA, this time in a coaching capacity. He signed as an assistant coach with the Los Angeles Clippers. Unfortunately, the hapless team failed to show significant improvement and he was not retained when the season ended.

As an assistant coach, Kareem Abdul-Jabbar shouts instructions from the Los Angeles Clippers bench.

Abdul-Jabbar finished his career with 38,387 points (24.6 points per game), nearly 7,000 more than Wilt Chamberlain, the next-highest scorer on the list. His 17,440 rebounds (11.2 rebounds per game), 3,189 blocks, and .559 field-goal percentage place him in the top ten on each career list. In addition to his six championship rings, six MVP awards, and two NBA Finals MVP awards, he was also a nineteen-time all-star, a two-time scoring champion, and a member of both the league's 35th and 50th Anniversary All-Time Teams. On May 15, 1995, Kareem received basketball's supreme accolade when he was enshrined in the Naismith Memorial Basketball Hall of Fame.

CHAPTER 6

Magic Johnson

M agic Johnson revolutionized the game of basketball as the
tallest point guard in history. He dazzled fans with his often
spectacular passes and led the Lakers to five NBA titles. Johnson's
contagious enthusiasm and love for the game, embodied in his infectious smile, was felt by all those who had the opportunity to
watch him perform on the court. Together with Boston's Larry Bird,
he is credited with helping to revive the NBA at a time when interest in the league was declining. As Bird himself once said, "Magic
is head and shoulders above everybody else. I've never seen [any-
body] as good as him." [69]

From Earvin to Magic

The boy who came to be called Magic was born Earvin Johnson Jr.
on August 14, 1959. He was the sixth of Earvin and Christine Johnson's ten children. The family lived in Lansing, Michigan, where
Earvin Sr. was an auto body worker at the General Motors plant.
Christine was a school custodian, and later a cafeteria supervisor.
With so many children, money was always tight, but the family
never lacked for love.

Earvin—or Junior—was a happy child. As his mother would say, "He's been this happy ever since he was knee-high to a duck."[70] He was nicknamed June Bug because he was constantly hopping around from one activity to another. Two of his favorite activities were singing and playing basketball. After receiving a basketball as a present, he slept with it at night.

Earvin "Magic" Johnson developed a love for basketball at a young age.

Johnson began playing basketball on the playgrounds of Lansing when he was in the sixth grade. He became obsessed with the sport and could often be found out on the court at 7:30 in the morning. He took a ball with him wherever he went. As he related in his autobiography, "No matter what else I was doing, I always had a basketball in my hand. If I was running an errand for my mother, I'd dribble on the way to the store. Just to make it interesting, I'd alternate right hand and left, block by block."[71]

By the time Earvin was ready for high school, he had made a name for himself at Dwight Rich Junior High. Because of race-based busing laws, he was forced to attend Everett High School, a white school on the south side of town. Despite feeling like an outsider, he led the Vikings to the Michigan Class A quarterfinals as a six-foot, five-inch sophomore, and to the semifinals as a junior. That year, as might be expected, the youngster apparently began to believe all the positive press he received for his performance and developed a cocky disposition. Johnson had to be threatened with a benching by his coach for his poor attitude. He would later call it "my wake-up call."[72]

The summer after his junior year, Magic's teammate and best friend, Reggie Chastaine, was killed in an auto accident. The team dedicated the season to him and promised to win the state title. Everett went 27–1 that year with Johnson averaging 28.8 points and 16.8 rebounds per game. Led by Johnson's 34 points and 14 rebounds in the championship game, the Vikings fulfilled their promise by winning an overtime thriller.

It was while at Everett that Johnson was given the nickname "Magic" by sportswriter Fred Stabley Jr. of the *Lansing State Journal*. Stabley had just seen Johnson score 36 points, pull down 18 rebounds, and pass off for 16 assists as a fifteen-year-old in a game against Jackson Parkside High School, a magical performance by any standards. Johnson's mother was not fond of the nickname. "When you say 'Magic,'" she said, "people expect so much. I was afraid that it would give him a lot to live up to at some point."[73]

As a result of high school celebrity, Magic was recruited by numerous colleges. He wanted to stay close to home, so he eventually decided on Michigan State University (MSU) in East Lansing. He majored in communications, with the goal of becoming a television broadcaster when his playing days were over.

Magic's presence revitalized the Michigan State Spartans basketball program.

Magic's presence at MSU revitalized the basketball program. As a six-foot, nine-inch freshman, Johnson led coach Jud Heathcote's squad to an impressive 25–5 record in 1977–78, and their first Big Ten title in nineteen years. He posted impressive totals, averaging 17 points, 7.9 rebounds, and 7.4 assists a game.

Magic did even better as a sophomore. He led the Spartans all the way to the final game of the NCAA Tournament, where they were matched up against Indiana State University and its star, Larry Bird. The game—which featured Bird, who had been voted Player of the Year in a vote of the nation's coaches, and Johnson, who had been runner-up—was one of the most publicized in NCAA Tournament annals. It was played before the largest national television audience ever to tune in to a college basketball game, and it ended in a 75–64 victory for the Spartans. Johnson

outscored Bird, 24 to 19, and was named the championship tournament's Most Outstanding Player. With a national title added to
his list of accomplishments, Magic was ready to take his game to
the next level of play. Still an underclassman, he soon declared
himself eligible for the NBA draft.

A Dream Come True

Johnson was selected as the first overall pick in the 1979 draft by
the Lakers. Magic was offered a contract calling for $600,000 a
year from "the only team [he] wanted to play for."[74] In his first
training camp that summer, he impressed the veterans with his
zest for the game. "He was so enthusiastic," recalled forward Ja-
maal Wilkes, "we couldn't believe he was for real."[75] In his first
regular season game, he went crazy after Kareem Abdul-Jabbar's
last-second shot gave the Lakers a win, acting as if they had won
the championship. The veteran center had to remind the rookie
that there were still eighty-one games remaining to be played.

Johnson's enthusiasm was infectious. He helped transform the
Lakers into an exciting, running team that moved into first place
in the league's Pacific Division. Magic dazzled everyone who saw
him, throwing full-court and no-look passes to cutting teammates.
In the words of David Israel of the *Chicago Tribune*, he "provided
the Lakers with leadership and spark and has turned them into
the most difficult kind of basketball team to contend with. . . .
They are a team with the most dominant of big men that plays a
running game."[76] (Most big men tend to be too slow to do well in
a running game.) In February 1980 he became the first rookie in
more than a decade to start in the NBA All-Star Game.

Johnson teamed with star center Kareem Abdul-Jabbar to lead
the Lakers into the playoffs where they breezed past the Phoenix
Suns and Seattle SuperSonics. In the NBA Finals, Los Angeles split
the first four games of the series with the Philadelphia 76ers. The
Lakers won Game 5, but Abdul-Jabbar injured his ankle and was
not available for the next contest, which would see Johnson give
one of the most memorable performances in league history.

Normally a point guard, Johnson was approached by Lakers'
coach Paul Westhead before the team boarded its plane for the
flight back to Philadelphia. "We'll need you to take over at center,"[77] he told Johnson. Magic agreed, and he dominated the game,

scoring 42 points (14 of 23 from the field and 14 of 14 from the foul line) with 15 rebounds, 7 assists, and 3 steals. "He has played center, forward, and guard in this game," said CBS broadcaster Brent Musburger as the contest neared its end. "He'll pack the uniforms afterward,"[78] Musberger joked. The Lakers won by a score of 123–107 and Johnson became the first rookie ever to be named

In one of the league's most memorable performances, rookie Magic Johnson led the Lakers to an NBA Championship.

MVP of the finals. The victory also made him the third player in history to win NCAA and NBA titles in successive seasons. Incredibly, it also gave him championships at three different levels (high school, college, and professional) in four seasons—all before he had reached his twenty-first birthday. Johnson was not, however, the league's Rookie of the Year. That honor went to Boston's Bird.

Johnson's second year in the league was interrupted by an injury, when Tom Burleson of the Atlanta Hawks fell on Magic's left knee. His importance to the team was never more evident. The Lakers were 15–5 when he went down. Magic was averaging more than 21 points a game and leading the league in assists and

Johnson drives up the court after returning from an injury that sidelined him for forty-five games.

steals. He missed forty-five games, but returned for the final six weeks of the regular season. "I was pleased with the way we carried on without him," said Coach Westhead. "But when Magic returned, it was like Looney Tunes. He created havoc. Everybody started laughing again."[79] Unfortunately for Los Angeles, the laughter died when the Lakers were upset by the Houston Rockets in the first round of the playoffs.

The summer of 1981, player salaries began to escalate as free agency became more common. With Magic having proved himself to be a vital component of the team, Lakers' owner Jerry Buss became fearful of the salary demands Johnson might make when his contract expired in 1984. In an unprecedented move, Buss signed his star to a twenty-five year extension worth $25 million. "I plan to make [Magic] my protege," announced Buss, "to teach him the business aspect of sports. I realize this is a very unusual contract because we're talking about a kid whose college class just graduated. But what it really comes down to is that Magic is part of the family."[80]

A New Regime

Though Johnson had been successful under Coach Westhead's system, he—along with several other Lakers players—began to feel constrained by the structured offense, with its set plays and slow pace. He reached a breaking point in November 1981 when he revealed his frustrated sentiments in a postgame tirade. "I can't play here anymore," he said. "I want to leave. I want to be traded."[81] Owner Buss had no intention of trading his young superstar, but he had been considering dismissing his coach and finally did, replacing him with the Lakers' assistant coach, Pat Riley. The widespread belief was that Johnson's demand for a trade was the impetus for Westhead's dismissal. Magic denied this, but his public image was tarnished. He heard boos at the Forum for the first time in his pro career. When the all-star balloting was held later that year, the fans failed to select him as a starter for only the second time in his career (the first was when he was injured).

The issue was eventually forgotten as his performance helped the team make it back to the playoffs. Johnson averaged 18.6 points per game while finishing second in the league in assists and leading in steals for the second year in a row. The Lakers swept both

Magic Johnson poses with his second Finals MVP award.

the Phoenix Suns and San Antonio Spurs in the postseason to march into the finals against the Philadelphia 76ers, their victims of two years before. For the second time in three years, Los Angeles defeated Philadelphia in six games, giving Magic the second championship ring of his brief three-year career, and his second Finals MVP award.

In the years that followed, Johnson was a model of consistency. From 1982–83 through 1986–87, his scoring increased each year. He also led the league in average assists per game each year, and total assists three times. The Lakers reached the NBA Finals in four of those five years, missing out only in 1985–86. They won championships in 1985 and 1987, defeating the Celtics in six-game series both years. With Boston having won in 1984, the Johnson-Bird rivalry continued—which had begun in college five years earlier.

The 1984 finals series was a low point in Johnson's career. He did not play especially well, and his poor performance at the end of Games 2, 4, and 7 played a key part in the losses. Some disappointed observers began calling him "Tragic" Johnson. He bounced back strongly, however, and so, too, did the Lakers. Beginning with the 1984–85 season, Los Angeles won NBA titles in three of the next four years. In 1987 and 1988, Magic helped the Lakers become the first club to win back-to-back championships since the 1968–69 Celtics.

In 1987 Johnson won the first of his three MVP awards. With Abdul-Jabbar sidelined for a portion of the year with an eye infection, the responsibility fell to Magic to become more of an offensive force. He responded by pouring in 23.9 points per game, the highest average of his pro career. That same season, he added his third Finals MVP trophy to his collection.

Johnson was the league's MVP in 1989, then again the next year. By the summer of 1990, however, the Lakers had changed dramatically. Abdul-Jabbar had retired, and Pat Riley stepped down as the team's coach. The club continued to win under a new coach, Mike Dunleavy, in 1991, but the team could not get past Michael Jordan and the Bulls in the finals.

A highlight of the 1991 season for Johnson occurred on April 15. On that day, he recorded assist number 9,888 to move past Oscar Robertson into first place on the NBA all-time list. It was barely six months after this historic event, however, that Magic received news that would dramatically change his life.

Devastating News

Under the terms of Johnson's contract with Los Angeles, he had to undergo a routine life-insurance physical. The results of the physical included tragic news—Johnson had tested positive for HIV, the virus that causes AIDS. On November 7, 1991, Magic revealed the results to the world. He added that on the advice of his doctor he was retiring, effective immediately, even though he was still in perfect physical condition. The reaction from fans and teammates was shock and disbelief.

After the diagnosis, Johnson dedicated himself to helping increase AIDS awareness around the country. He helped raise money for research and tried to educate people on the disease and its consequences. For his tireless work and contributions to the community, he was presented with the NBA's J. Walter Kennedy Citizenship Award.

Despite his retirement, Magic found it difficult to stay away from the game he loved. He was voted as a starter to

After being diagnosed with HIV, Johnson dedicated himself to help increase AIDS awareness.

the All-Star Game that season and decided to play. He won the game's MVP award by scoring 25 points and recording 9 assists. (In eleven career all-star appearances, he averaged 16 points and 11.5 assists per game.) Later that summer, he was named to the U.S. Olympic basketball squad, the first such team on which professional players were allowed to play. The "Dream Team," as it was called, competed in the summer games in Barcelona, Spain, and brought home gold medals.

His play in Barcelona encouraged Johnson to attempt a comeback in the NBA that fall. He played several exhibition games, but

Magic Johnson briefly returned from retirement after being named to the U.S. Olympic "Dream Team."

gave up the idea when some players expressed concern about playing against someone who had tested HIV positive. They mistakenly believed they were in danger of becoming infected by coming in contact with him.

Without their all-star guard to lead them, the Lakers struggled through the 1991–92 and 1992–93 seasons. When they again showed a losing record the next year, owner Jerry Buss fired head coach Randy Pfund, who had taken over for Dunleavy in 1992, and hired Johnson as his replacement. Magic was unsuccessful as a coach. The team won just five of sixteen games with him at the helm and failed to make the playoffs for the first time since the 1975–76 season. Johnson quit at the end of the season, and it appeared his NBA journey was finally over. "It's never been my dream to coach," he said. "I want to own, to be a businessman. You've got to chase your dreams."[82]

Two years later, however, at the age of thirty-six, Magic made one final comeback. By this time, an influx of young players had given the Lakers a renewed hope for the championship. In addition, players had become better informed, and fears of playing with or against someone who had tested positive for HIV had subsided. Johnson rejoined the team on January 30 and scored 19 points with 8 rebounds and 10 assists in his first game back. Although he averaged an impressive 15.3 points, 8.5 rebounds, and 6.5 assists over the last thirty-two games of the season, he could sense that the team chemistry had been disrupted by his return and the publicity it generated. He retired for the last time following the team's first-round playoff loss to the Houston Rockets. "I am going out on my terms," said Magic, "something I couldn't say when I aborted a comeback in 1992."[83]

Since his retirement, Johnson has taken on new ventures. He has a burgeoning business empire—Magic Johnson Enterprises (MJE)—composed of a number of subsidiaries, including Magic Johnson Theatres, a chain of multiplex movie theaters in many of the country's major cities. His other holdings include a Las Vegas shopping center, and Starbucks and TGI Friday's franchises.

Magic also founded the Magic Johnson Foundation in 1991. The nonprofit organization works toward improving the quality of life of inner-city youths. He gives countless hours of his time to the community and assists many charities in raising funds. The U.S.

Magic founded the Magic Johnson Foundation in 1991 to improve the quality of life for inner-city youths.

National AIDS Committee, the United Negro College Fund, the Muscular Dystrophy Association, the American Heart Association, and the Urban League are just a few that have benefited from his involvement.

On the basketball court, Johnson will always be remembered for his ballhandling and passing skills, which had never before been seen in someone his height. He retired with the second-highest assist total in league history. Magic's all-around play inspired a new, unofficial statistic, the "triple-double" (reaching a total of ten in any three categories—usually points, rebounds, and assists—in a single game). He finished with 138 triple-doubles, second on the career list to Oscar Robertson's earlier 178.

Numbers alone, however, do not tell the full story of Johnson's impact on the game of basketball. With his wide, bright smile, Magic was a walking advertisement for the game he loved. As he once said, "There is a time for business and a time for fun. Basketball is fun."[84] Bringing that joy to everyone who saw him play is perhaps his greatest achievement of all.

CHAPTER 7

Pat Riley

Pat Riley is likely the most celebrated and recognized basketball coach in the world. He compiled an enviable record with each team he commanded in his NBA career, beginning with the Lakers, and continuing with the Knicks and Miami Heat. Pacing the sidelines in his Armani suits, the suave, handsome "Riles" was the ideal high-profile coach to lead the Showtime Lakers to four championships in his tenure with the team.

A Child of the Fifties

Born in Rome, New York, on March 20, 1945, Patrick James Riley was the youngest of three sons and six children born to Leon "Lee" Riley and his wife, Mary. Lee had played major league baseball briefly with the Philadelphia Phillies (four games in 1944), and was a manager in the team's minor league farm system. His sons inherited their athletic tendencies from their father. In addition to Pat, son Lee Jr. also played professional sports as a defensive back with three teams in the National Football League (NFL) and the New York Titans in the American Football League (AFL).

When Pat was a young child, the family moved frequently as Lee Sr. pursued his dream of making it back to the major leagues as a

As a coach, Pat Riley became a master of discipline despite his rebellious past.

manager. The dream never materialized, however. After being released from the minors in 1952, he and his family finally settled in Schenectady in the eastern part of New York State. There, he ran a restaurant-bar and a convenience store.

As a youngster, Pat was the stereotypical rebel child of the 1950s, a "greased-hair, cigarette-pack-in-the-sleeve adolescent,"[85] as described by Roy S. Johnson in the *New York Times.* He had been expelled from a Catholic boarding school when he was eight and had several brushes with the law. As he confessed to Johnson, "I once broke forty-five or fifty windows in my junior high school and, later, broke into the cafeteria and ate all the ice cream."[86] Getting caught made Riley realize he had to change his ways. He channeled his energies into basketball and began to be recognized as an athlete.

Learning His Lessons

Pat's father encouraged his boys' involvement in athletics. To condition Pat for the more physical aspect of sports, Lee instructed his older sons to take their brother to the less privileged Lincoln Heights section of Schenectady to play against some tougher kids. "I would get beat up, knocked around," said Riley. "I would run home crying."[87] The reason for the directive, according to Lee, was to teach his son not to be afraid of rough competition.

Another person who helped Riley complete his transformation was Walt Pazybylo, the basketball coach at Linton High School in Schenectady. A strict disciplinarian, Pazybylo insisted Riley follow his rules. He instilled in the youngster his theories on basketball as well as his philosophy of life. "Walt really took Pat under his wing," said Riley's former high school teammate Mike Meola. "He cared about all his players, but you could tell how he felt about Pat and it was mutual. Pat was looking for someone like him."[88]

Riley excelled at every sport he tried. As a senior, he was the starting quarterback on the football team, and the star six-foot, two-inch forward on the basketball squad. The highlight of his basketball career at Linton occurred during his junior year. Linton played New York's mighty Power Memorial squad in the Schenectady Holiday Festival. Power was led by its freshman prodigy, six-foot, ten-inch sensation Lew Alcindor. Linton won as Riley outscored Alcindor, 19 to 8, something he would not hesitate to remind Alcindor (now Kareem Abdul-Jabbar) about when he coached him with the Lakers.

His high school success helped Riley attract the attention of numerous college coaches. He turned down an opportunity to play football at Alabama for Bear Bryant. Instead, he opted to go to the University of Kentucky and play basketball for the Wildcats' legendary coach, Adolph Rupp.

Riley fit in well with Rupp's style of play, which emphasized a pressing defense and fast-breaking offense. Because of his ballhandling skills and shooting ability, he was switched to the guard position. Riley responded well to Rupp's dictatorial approach. "He was a great, great presence," says Riley. "I take basically a lot of my philosophy from his coaching. I had four years of a drill-type mentality."[89]

After finishing with a 15–10 record in Riley's first season on the varsity,

Riley's basketball success in high school secured a position at the University of Kentucky.

the Wildcats advanced all the way to the championship game of the NCAA Tournament in his junior year of 1965–66. They lost to Texas Western University in what is recognized today as a landmark game. It marked the first time an all-black squad defeated an all-white one for the title.

Riley averaged 22 points per game that season, and he was voted the team's most valuable player and a first-team all-American. A back injury kept him from duplicating those numbers as a senior, but he was still named first-team All-Southeastern Conference. When it came time for the 1967 NBA draft, Riley was the first draft pick of the San Diego Rockets, a new expansion team. Even though he had not played football since high school, he was a good enough athlete to also warrant being chosen in the eleventh round of the NFL draft by the Dallas Cowboys. Basketball was his preference, however, and he signed with the Rockets.

The Role Player

Like many players who were stars in college, Riley did not attain the same level as a pro. After three seasons with San Diego, he was made available in the 1970 expansion draft. He was selected by the Portland Trail Blazers, but never played for the team. Following an exhibition game against the Lakers, Riley approached Chick Hearn, the Lakers' broadcaster and former assistant general manager who still had considerable influence with Lakers' owner Jack Kent Cooke. "You've got to get me out of here,"[90] begged Riley, not looking forward to playing with another expansion team. Hearn suggested the move to management, and when Portland released the unhappy Riley just prior to the start of the 1970–71 season, he was signed by the Lakers.

With Los Angeles, Riley was a backup to starting guard Jerry West. In this role, he gained a measure of success on the 1971–72 Lakers squad, that won thirty-three games in a row and the NBA championship. When West retired following the 1973–74 season, Riley moved into the starting rotation. He had his best year as a pro, averaging 11 points a game as Gail Goodrich's partner in the Lakers' backcourt.

In November 1975 Riley was traded to the Phoenix Suns after suffering a leg injury that required surgery. Riley was crushed. "I felt betrayed," he said later. "My only pro blood is Laker blood. They were the only team I cared about or had a passion for. As a role-player, you have to keep your problems internal. But I was so angry that I couldn't even see the game."[91]

Riley's emotional level plunged even further when he was released by Phoenix the following May. He sank into a depression that he eventually came out of with the help of his wife, Chris, a psychologist. "Pat was at a very vulnerable time," she explained. "His playing career had just ended, and he was going through all the fears men went through in the seventies."[92] Riley agreed. "It was a period of mourning," he said. "Basketball was my whole life."[93] To help him get through this difficult period,

Pat Riley moved into the starting position for the Lakers after Jerry West retired.

Riley began writing about his thoughts and feelings toward the game. The resulting seven-hundred-page work helped him come to peace with himself and helped him maintain his sanity.

Just over a year after he was released, he was contacted by Lakers' broadcaster Chick Hearn, who offered Riley the opportunity to join his broadcasting team. Riley accepted and remained in the position for two years.

When Paul Westhead took over the reins as the Lakers' head coach fourteen games into the 1979–80 season, he asked Riley to join his staff as an assistant. Westhead's regime lasted just two years before he was fired. Riley was hired as his replacement despite owner Jerry Buss's concerns about his inexperience. At a hastily called news conference, Buss actually named Riley and Jerry West as cocoaches. West, however, was not interested in the position. He handed the microphone to Riley saying that his own role would be an advisory position.

The Master Motivator

Riley took his work seriously. "I didn't know how to lead people," he said of that 1981–82 season. "I didn't have any file cabinet full of ideas about how to get things done. . . . So I read and I talked to people in leadership positions. I had to work."[94] Riley was a fast learner and allowed his players more freedom than they had under Westhead's tightly controlled system. The Lakers responded by finishing the regular season in first place in the Pacific Division. In the playoffs, they swept the Phoenix Suns and San Antonio Spurs in four games each to get to the NBA Finals. There, they subdued the Philadelphia 76ers in six games to take the championship.

Having won a title in his very first year, Riley's expectations were high as he began his second season in charge. He worked as hard at coaching as he had at playing, doing everything he could to motivate his players into giving their best, night after night.

Riley's coaching style allowed more freedom for his players.

Unfortunately, injuries plagued the team. Although the club made it to the final series once again, this time the 76ers got their revenge by defeating the Lakers in four straight games.

The next year, Riley's club made it to the finals for the third time in three years. The Lakers' opponents this time were the Celtics. The two teams played seven hard-fought contests with Boston winning four of them, including two in overtime. The defeat was one of the bitterest of Riley's career. "In 1984," he said, "we had the best team and flat out choked when we lost to Boston."[95]

The Celtics and Lakers met in the finals again the next season. Riley and his team were determined to make up for the previous year's disappointment. They started out poorly, however, getting trounced in the opening game in Boston—a game that would be be remembered as the Memorial Day Massacre—by a score of 148—114. With Game 2 also being played in the Boston Garden, the Lakers faced a daunting task. Another loss would give the Celtics a two-games-to-none lead, a margin seldom overcome in championship series play.

The Lakers, however, were up to the challenge. They won Game 2, 109–102, which evened the series. Riley would later say, "That was the most significant game this team ever played. If we had lost it, I'm sure I'd have been fired and people would have been traded. . . . It was the ultimate backs against the wall. . . . And it brought out the best."[96] Los Angeles won three of the next four games to wrest the title away from the Celtics and give Riley his second championship ring. It marked the ninth time the two teams met in the finals and the first time the Lakers emerged on top.

The victory demonstrated the validity of Riley's coaching philosophy and his ability to inspire his players. He challenged them to compete against themselves in practice every day. One of his principal teachings is that you receive only what you are willing to give. To become a champion, you must be willing to sacrifice and to be selfless. The Lakers followed this mantra, and the result was an NBA title.

The difficulty involved in maintaining that high level of dedication was seen in the 1985–86 season. The Lakers finished the regular season with the second-best record in the league at 62–20. They defeated the Dallas Mavericks in the Western Conference Semifinals, then beat the Houston Rockets in the first game of the

Conference Finals. The underdog Rockets had finished the year with a 51–31 mark and figured to be no match for Los Angeles.

Surprisingly, the Rockets swept the next four games to bring the Lakers' season to a screeching halt. The final game was decided on a miraculous shot at the buzzer by Houston's Ralph Sampson, giving the Rockets a 114–112 win. The loss was a tremendous disappointment for Riley. "We thought we'd win easily," he explained, "and we started to get away from our philosophy of speed and quickness. . . . We got away from running and attacking."[97] Overconfidence, in other words, had made them get away from the basics that had led to their success.

In an attempt to correct the team's flaws, Riley promised to allow the Lakers more offensive freedom, using more improvisation and fewer set plays. To do this, he passed the mantle of leadership from thirty-nine-year-old center Kareem Abdul-Jabbar to twenty-seven-year-old guard Magic Johnson. The results were impressive.

The Guarantee

The Lakers improved their record to 65–17 in 1986–87 and advanced to the finals, where they played the Boston Celtics once again. The Lakers won the series in six games, giving Riley his third championship in six years. As the players celebrated in the locker room after the game, someone asked the coach if his team could win again the next year. Rather than give the standard noncommittal answer the question usually generates, Riley stunned his players. "I'm going to guarantee it," he declared, "we're going to win the thing again next year."[98]

Many of Riley's players later admitted that his pronouncement helped them the next season. "Guaranteeing a championship was the best thing Pat ever did," said guard Byron Scott. "It set the stage in our minds. Work harder, be better. That's the only way we could repeat."[99] It was Riley's belief that his team needed some extra motivation if it wanted to be ranked with the greatest teams in history. "Even though the Lakers had won four championships in the 80s by then," he explained, "I felt they were never going to get the credit for really, truly being a great team until they took responsibility for the criteria on which they were going to be judged: winning back-to-back."[100]

*After the 1986–87 finals, Riley stunned his players by guaranteeing a
championship for the next year.*

Throughout the year, Riley did not let his team forget his guarantee. The Lakers responded by beginning the 1987–88 season
winning their first eight games. They later compiled a fifteen-
game streak. Los Angeles won the Pacific Division title for a
record seventh consecutive time, forging a 62–20 record. The San
Antonio Spurs were no match for the Lakers in the opening round
of the playoffs, falling in three straight games. The Utah Jazz (who
had relocated from New Orleans), Dallas Mavericks, and Detroit
Pistons, however, proved to be more of a test. Each of the three
teams stretched the Lakers to the limit, dragging its series out to
seven games before succumbing. Riley's prophecy had come true.
The Lakers had repeated as champs, winning the title for the
fourth—and last—time under his command.

Time for a Change

The Lakers won the Pacific Division title again in the 1988–89 season, but their quest for a third consecutive NBA crown was derailed by the Pistons, who swept them in four straight games in the finals series. The following season, they recorded the best regular season record in the league (63–19), earning Riley his first NBA Coach of the Year award. In the Western Conference Semifinals, however, the Lakers were upset by a tough Phoenix Suns team.

Over the years, Riley had used various methods to motivate his team to perform at its best. These included his use of "TIs," or fits of temporary insanity. They involved "being angry at the right time, to the right degree, at the right people."[101] After nine

Riley's coaching methods relied on "being angry at the right time, to the right degree, at the right people."

years, however, his speeches and tricks had lost much of their effectiveness and his manner began to irritate his players more and more. Few could handle his intense manner and insistence on complete authority. By that point, recounted one player, "he didn't have a friend left in the locker room."[102]

Riley knew it was time to move on to a new challenge. He stepped down as the Lakers' coach on June 11, 1990. Riley had compiled a 533–194 record in his nine seasons with the Lakers. He led Los Angeles to nine consecutive Pacific Division titles, and never posted fewer than fifty victories in a season.

After working as a broadcaster for NBC Sports for one year, Riley returned to the coaching wars when he signed with the Knicks in 1991. He coached New York for four years and extended his streak of division titles to twelve consecutive before finishing in second place in 1994–95. He helped revive a floundering Knicks franchise, averaging nearly fifty-six wins a year in his tenure as coach. The closest he came to winning another title was in 1994, when he led the team to the NBA Finals. There they lost a hard-fought seven-game series to the Houston Rockets.

After the 1994–95 season, Riley resigned with one year remaining on his contract. He accepted an offer from the Miami Heat to become a part-owner of the team as well as its head coach. In his sixth season with the Heat, he has extended his streak of winning seasons to nineteen, with his teams having made the playoffs in each one. On November 1, 2000, he reached a coaching milestone by recording the one thousandth win of his NBA career.

Riley's success as a coach has led him to other fields. He has become one of the most sought-after motivational speakers in the country, rated by *Success* magazine as one of the best in the field. His understanding of the dynamics necessary for developing a successful team can be applied to the corporate—as well as the athletic—environment. He is also the author of *The Winner Within: A Life Plan for Team Players*.

Riley's motivational skills helped him compile impressive statistics in his years as a head coach. He guided teams to 1,049 wins as of 2001, second on the NBA's all-time list. He also ranks first in career playoff wins. He will likely someday take his place among the game's immortals in the Naismith Memorial Basketball Hall of Fame.

CHAPTER 8

Shaquille O'Neal

Shaquille O'Neal is the dominant force in professional basketball today. At seven-feet, one-inch tall and 330 pounds, he is a larger-than-life figure in the entertainment capital of the world. In addition to leading the Lakers to their most recent championship in 2001, he has taken advantage of the opportunities offered by Los Angeles to establish himself in the fields of movies and music.

An Army Brat

On March 6, 1972, Lucille O'Neal of Newark, New Jersey, gave birth to a boy to whom she gave the Islamic name Shaquille Rashaun. In Arabic, the name translates to "little warrior." "I wanted my children to have unique names," she said. "To me, just by having a name that means something makes you special."[103] Little did she know how special her little warrior would grow up to be.

The boy's father, Joseph Toney, soon abandoned his family and eventually ended up in jail. The young mother worked two jobs trying to provide for her family while her son was cared for by relatives. When Shaquille was two years old, Lucille's position as a city worker brought her into contact with a man named Philip A. Harrison. The couple soon married and Harrison adopted

Shaquille as his own son. Lucille and Philip had three other children: sons Ayesha and Jamal, and daughter Lateefah. Harrison was a strict disciplinarian, but he was loved and respected by Shaquille, who calls Harrison his true father. As he explained years later, "When my mother needed someone twenty-one years ago, Phil Harrison was the man. He is my dad. He's the one who raised me and made me what I am today."[104]

To get out of the crime-ridden streets of Newark and provide a better life for his family, Harrison decided to make the army his career. The job paid well, but forced him to travel across the country and around the world. By the time Shaquille was a teenager, he had already lived on army bases in New Jersey, Germany, Georgia, and Texas.

Adjusting to life in new towns was difficult for the youngster, who was growing at a rapid rate. "The worst part was the traveling," said O'Neal. "Meeting people, getting tight with them, and

With the name that translates to "little warrior," Shaquille Rashaun O'Neal seemed destined for greatness.

then having to leave. . . . I was teased a lot—teased about my name, teased about my size. . . . Because of that, I got in a lot of fights and it sometimes took me a while to make new friends." [105] Shaquille began associating with bad influences, which led to all sorts of trouble. "I was bad," he confessed. "I stole. I lied. I cheated. I broke into cars to steal tapes." [106]

Shaquille's father realized the boy needed a healthy interest to occupy his time, so he introduced him to basketball. At the time, Sergeant Harrison was stationed in Fulda, Germany. While there, he heard about a clinic that was to be given by Louisiana State University head basketball coach Dale Brown. The six-foot, six-inch, thirteen-year-old Shaquille attended the seminar and made quite an impression on Brown, one that Brown would not forget.

Shortly after that meeting, Shaquille's father was transferred once again, this time to Fort Sam Houston in San Antonio, Texas. Shaquille enrolled at Robert G. Cole High School on the base and played on the school's basketball team. As a junior, he dominated play right from the start, leading the Cougars to an undefeated regular season. The next year, he averaged 32 points, 22 rebounds, and 8 blocked shots a game. Cole went 36–0 on its way to the 1989 state championship in its division, with O'Neal named as a *Parade* magazine all-American.

By this time, Shaquille had grown to six-feet, eleven-inches tall and weighed 270 pounds. Players his size were rare. His size and talent attracted the attention of more than a hundred colleges and universities. His work ethic was just as important as his natural abilities. "Shaquille was always one of the hardest workers on the team," said Cole assistant coach Herb More. "Whether on the court or in the weight room, he always gave me the feeling that he wanted to improve all the time, wanted to be the best in everything he did." [107] When it was time for him to make a decision, O'Neal decided to attend Louisiana State University (LSU). He had kept in touch with Dale Brown over the years and knew he wanted to play for the Tigers.

As the largest—and most publicized—recruit in LSU's history, O'Neal was the center of attention right from the start. Because of this, Coach Brown was careful to bring him along slowly. In his freshman season, O'Neal averaged just under 14 points and 12 rebounds per game. On defense he averaged more than 3 blocked shots per contest.

The next season, LSU's star guard Chris Jackson left to play in the NBA. Its other star, Stanley Roberts, was declared academically ineligible. O'Neal became the focal point of the team and blossomed as a player. He averaged 27.6 points and 14.7 rebounds a game and won the Adolph Rupp Award as the National Player of the Year. Against Arkansas State University, he scored a school-record 53 points while taking down 19 rebounds and blocking 5 shots.

O'Neal disregarded predictions that he would leave school to enter the NBA draft. He was having too much fun enjoying college life. In his junior year he continued to improve. Opposing teams were frustrated. Knowing they could not stop the seven-foot-tall O'Neal, they double- and triple-teamed him and constantly hacked at his body. Despite his size and strength, the constant pounding began to take its toll. In one game, he threw an elbow at an opponent who blatantly fouled him, precipitating a brawl. O'Neal was thrown out of the contest and suspended for a game.

O'Neal finished the year with an average of 24.1 points per game. He also finished second in the nation in rebounding and first in blocked shots. Because of the rough treatment the star had encountered, however, Coach Brown reached a decision. He advised O'Neal to turn pro rather than stay at LSU and risk a career-ending injury. O'Neal agreed and announced his decision to the press in early April 1992. He was ready to move on to the next stage of his career.

The Magic Kingdom

O'Neal was the obvious choice as the top overall pick in the 1992 draft. Under the NBA's lottery system, the eleven teams that failed to make the playoffs the previous season had a chance at getting him. Ping-pong balls with each team's name were put in a barrel. After they were mixed, the balls were randomly selected to determine the order in which the teams would pick. On May 17, 1992, a television audience watched as the first ball picked carried the name of the Orlando Magic. Magic general manager Pat Williams smiled, knowing Orlando would use the pick to take Shaquille Rashaun O'Neal.

Just over a month later, on June 24, the team made it official. At a press conference in Orlando shortly after the draft, O'Neal addressed the local media. "I feel fortunate to get picked by Orlando," he said. "I'm not promising a championship the first year. Things take time. But I'll learn the ropes, get my feet wet, and become a good player."[108]

Orlando signed O'Neal to a lucrative seven-year contract worth $40 million. That summer, in an effort to improve himself, he spent time at a special camp for big men held by former college coach Pete Newell, where Shaq was taught the intricacies of playing the center position. "He came here voluntarily," said Newell, "and that really says something about the kid. . . . I'm very impressed by him. He's amazingly agile for his size, very explosive. He has to rank already with any of the great centers."[109]

Picking first in the 1992 draft, Orlando selected Shaq, who signed for $40 million.

Shaq began to show his value right away. In his first regular season game, he scored 12 points and pulled down 18 rebounds against the Miami Heat. He improved rapidly and by the end of his first week, he was averaging 26 points and 16 rebounds a game. He was named the league's Player of the Week and Player of the Month. It was the first time in NBA history that a rookie had won those awards immediately upon entering the league. Many observers believed O'Neal had the biggest impact on the league of any rookie since Wilt Chamberlain more than three decades before. That February, fans voted Shaq to the NBA All-Star Game. At age twenty, he was the youngest all-star ever. O'Neal scored 14 points and pulled down 7 rebounds in the East's 135–132 overtime loss to the West.

By the end of the year, the Magic had nearly doubled their number of wins from the previous season (from twenty-one to forty-one). O'Neal averaged 23.4 points, 13.9 rebounds, and 3.5 blocked shots per game for the year. In Rookie of the Year balloting, Shaq received ninety-

Shaq dedicates much of his free time to children and the less fortunate.

six of ninety-eight possible votes to take the award. "I'm very happy and very proud to win this," he said of the honor. "It's been a long year, but I learned a lot and I'm already looking forward to next season." [110]

Shaq loved the attention that was showered on him. He was like an overgrown kid living out a childlike fantasy. He was a frequent guest on television shows and met many entertainment celebrities. Shortly after the season ended, the music-loving Shaq cut his first hip-hop album, *Shaq Diesel*, as well as a video for MTV.

At the same time, however, O'Neal was showing an appreciation for all he had received. He spent much of his spare time visiting patients in children's hospitals and donating thousands of dollars worth of toys. He also helped feed people at an Orlando homeless shelter and bought turkeys for many underprivileged families at Thanksgiving.

Despite his impressive debut, O'Neal was determined to improve. He was, after all, just twenty-one years old. Shaq especially needed work on his free-throw shooting and on avoiding fouls. In an effort to improve, he again spent two weeks at Newell's camp to work on his inside moves.

The Magic also looked to improve. They signed rookie Anfernee "Penny" Hardaway to play point guard and pass the ball to O'Neal. With Hardaway directing the action from the outside and O'Neal dominating play on the inside, the Magic felt they now had the pieces in place to make a run for a spot in the playoffs.

O'Neal's second season was even more impressive than his first. He finished second in the league in both scoring and rebounding. Led by O'Neal and Hardaway, the Magic made the playoffs for the first time in their history in 1993–94, but they were eliminated in the first round by the Indiana Pacers.

That summer, O'Neal spent more time on basketball and less on his outside activities. He played on the U.S. national team at the World Championships in Toronto, Canada. Following that, he worked on improving his foul shooting with well-known coach Buzz Braman, and again spent more time with Pete Newell. Shaq's desire was to lead the Magic to a championship. He was determined to do everything possible to achieve that goal.

O'Neal's hard work paid off. The Magic finished atop the NBA's Atlantic Division in 1994–95 with a record of 57–25, including an incredible 39–2 at home in the Orlando Arena. Shaq led the league in scoring with an average of just under 30 points per game. He also finished second in shooting percentage, third in rebounds, and sixth in blocked shots.

In the postseason, O'Neal played like a man possessed, determined to help the team make up for its poor playoff showing the year before. To accomplish this, he had to defeat the latest strategy used by opposing teams to stop him. This strategy—called the "Hack-a-Shaq" by Orlando coach Brian Hill—called for the opposition to foul O'Neal every time he got the ball down deep near the basket. This strategy prevented him from scoring on an easy two-point shot, forcing him to convert free throws, which were still one of his weaknesses.

The Celtics tried this maneuver but were unsuccessful as the Magic swept past them in four games. Michael Jordan and the Chicago Bulls were next, but Orlando dispatched them in six games. In the Division Finals, the Magic faced the Indiana Pacers, who had ended the Magic's season the previous year. This time, as Shaq promised, he had improved. O'Neal averaged 31 points per game over the seven contests and the Magic prevailed, moving into the NBA Finals against the defending champion Houston Rockets. They were swept in four straight games by the Rockets, however, thus coming up short in their quest for a title.

California, Here He Comes

The frustration of 1995 became even worse the following season. O'Neal's grandmother died in midseason, and his departure for the funeral created a rift between Shaq and team management. He felt he should have been allowed as much time away from the team as

he needed, but the Magic felt he could have returned sooner. Several of his teammates were also disappointed in his attitude, but he felt the same way about their lack of support.

The situation added to the doubts some people had about O'Neal's ability to lead the team. The talk increased when the playoffs came around and the Magic was swept by Michael Jordan and the Chicago Bulls. With his contract about to expire, O'Neal announced that he would not re-sign with the team for less than $150 million. The Magic offered him $69 million over seven years. Eventually Shaq signed with the Lakers as a free agent for $121 million.

O'Neal's first three seasons with Los Angeles were no more successful than those with Orlando. The team compiled good records each year, but they never made it to the

Frustrated with Orlando, Shaq made a move west, signing with the Lakers.

final round of the playoffs. There was dissension between the coaches and players—and among the players themselves—about how the team was being run. When Shaq believed that special attention was given to Kobe Bryant, who joined the team directly out of high school in 1996, the situation worsened. A series of injuries added to O'Neal's woes, making his dream of a championship seem as distant as ever.

The dream, however, became real again prior to the start of the 1999–2000 season, when Los Angeles hired former Bulls' coach Phil Jackson to lead the team. Jackson's no-nonsense manner reminded O'Neal of his father. Shaq knew it was exactly what the Lakers needed.

O'Neal and the Lakers responded positively to Jackson's guiding hand. The team won sixty-seven games and lost just fifteen to take first place in the Pacific Division. O'Neal dominated play the entire year. He ranked first in the league in points per game (29.7), first in field-goal percentage (.574), second in rebounds per game (13.6), and third in blocks per game (3.03). In addition to being named All-NBA First Team and All-Defensive Second Team, he was the nearly unanimous choice for MVP. The difference in his play could be seen by legendary former UCLA coach John Wooden. "Prior to last year I thought he was just a dunker," said the Hall of Fame mentor, "but this year his court vision got better, he shared the ball willingly and I thought he showed more moves around the basket, so I'd have to say he's more of a complete player than before." [111]

In the playoffs, the Lakers defeated the Sacramento Kings in five games, the Phoenix Suns in five, and the Portland Trail Blazers in seven. Los Angeles met the Indiana Pacers in the finals series, and with Shaq leading the way, won four games to two to take the championship. By averaging 38 points and 16.7 rebounds per game against Indiana, O'Neal added the NBA Finals MVP award to his trophy case. At long last, his quest for a championship was realized.

A Giant Future

Not yet thirty years of age, Shaquille O'Neal has accomplished many things in his young life. In addition to his success in the pro

Shaq slams the ball, leading the Lakers to a NBA championship in the 1999–2000 season.

ranks, he also brought home an Olympic gold medal as a member of the 1996 U.S. "Dream Team" that competed in Atlanta, Georgia. Off the court, he has made four more rap albums since his first *Shaq Fu: Da Return; You Can't Stop the Reign; Respect;* and a greatest hits album. He starred in the movies *Kazaam* and *Steel* and also made an appearance in the movie *Blue Chips*. Shaq is also an entrepreneur; he owns his own record label and a sportswear company, TWIsM, Inc. (This World Is Mine). The success of his many endeavors has also allowed him to give much back to the community, particularly to disadvantaged children.

Shaq starred in the movie Kazaam, *one of his many off-the-court endeavors.*

Despite his many accomplishments, O'Neal found the time to carry through on a promise he made to his mother when he left LSU in 1992. At the time, he vowed to return someday to get his degree. In the eight intervening years, he attended some classes during the summer, and earned credits through LSU's independent studies program. On December 15, 2000, he received his bachelor of arts in general studies with a minor in political science.

The future remains bright for O'Neal, with new challenges awaiting him. After the 2000 title, Lakers' assistant coach Tex Winter said, "No one man can stop him, and you can't play a zone, so I guess they figure with enough big bodies they'll just wear him down, but Shaquille loves a challenge, so it'll be interesting."[112] In the spring of 2001, however, the NBA changed the rules. For the 2001–02 season, the zone defense will be allowed, with the intent of cutting down on isolation plays (where one side of the court is cleared out while a single player goes one-on-one against a single defender). With the zone defense legal, it will be possible to double- and triple-team big men like O'Neal to cut down on their effectiveness around the basket. How Shaq responds to the new rule will be one of the interesting stories of the new year. His ability to cope will be a significant factor in whether or not the Lakers are able to maintain their standing in the NBA's upper echelon of teams.

Notes

Chapter 1: From the Land of Lakes

1. Quoted in Peter C. Bjarkman, *The Encyclopedia of Pro Basketball Team Histories*. New York: Carroll & Graf Publishers, 1994, p. 52.
2. Quoted in Stew Thornley, "Game with 12-Foot Baskets," University of Minnesota, www.tc.umn.edu/~thorn017/mplslakers_12foot.html.
3. Quoted in Thornley, "Game with 12-Foot Baskets."
4. Quoted in Tim Crothers, *Greatest Teams: The Most Dominant Powerhouses in Sports*. New York: Time, 1998, p. 76.

Chapter 2: George Mikan

5. Quoted in Alexander Wolff, *Basketball: A History of the Game*. New York: Time, 1997, p. 132.
6. Quoted in Lee Enderlin, "The Big Number 99," *Sports History*, March 1990, p. 30.
7. Quoted in Enderlin, "The Big Number 99," p. 26.
8. Quoted in Ron Fimrite, "Big George," *Sports Illustrated*, November 6, 1989, p. 136.
9. Quoted in Fimrite, "Big George," p. 137.
10. Quoted in Crothers, *Greatest Teams*, p. 95.
11. Quoted in "George Mikan," National Basketball Association, www.global.nba.com/history/mikan_bio.html.
12. Quoted in Dan Barreiro, "Before Wilt, Kareem and Shaq, There Was Mikan," *Minneapolis-St. Paul Star Tribune*, www.thesunlink.com/news/99december/daily1223cld.html.
13. Quoted in Barreiro, "Before Wilt, Kareem and Shaq, There Was Mikan."
14. Quoted in Barreiro, "Before Wilt, Kareem and Shaq, There Was Mikan."
15. Quoted in "George Mikan," National Basketball Association.

16. Quoted in Ron Fimrite, "Big George," p. 139.
17. Quoted in "George Mikan," National Basketball Association.
18. Quoted in "George Mikan," National Basketball Association.
19. Quoted in Wolff, *Basketball*, p. 132.
20. Quoted in Fimrite, "Big George," p. 140.

Chapter 3: Elgin Baylor

21. Quoted in Wolff, *Basketball*, p. 118.
22. Quoted in Larry Schwartz, "Before Michael, There Was Elgin," ESPN, www.espn.go.com/sportscentury/features/00014086.html.
23. Quoted in Frank Deford, "A Tiger Who Could Beat Anything," *Sports Illustrated*, March 28, 2000, www.sportsillustrated.cnn.com/features/cover/news/2000/03/27/baylor_deford.
24. Quoted in Schwartz, "Before Michael, There Was Elgin."
25. Quoted in Schwartz, "Before Michael, There Was Elgin."
26. Quoted in Deford, "A Tiger Who Could Beat Anything."
27. Quoted in "Elgin Baylor," NBA, www.global.nba.com/history/baylor_bio.html.
28. Quoted in "Baylor Hits 61 in the Finals," NBA, www.global.nba.com/nbaat50/moments/baylor_61.html.
29. Quoted in "Baylor Hits 61 in the Finals," NBA.
30. Quoted in Deford, "A Tiger Who Could Beat Anything."
31. Quoted in Deford, "A Tiger Who Could Beat Anything."
32. Quoted in Schwartz, "Before Michael, There Was Elgin."
33. Quoted in Deford, "A Tiger Who Could Beat Anything."
34. Quoted in Deford, "A Tiger Who Could Beat Anything."
35. Quoted in Steve Springer, *The Los Angeles Times Encyclopedia of the Lakers*. Los Angeles: Los Angeles Times, 1998, p. 25.
36. Quoted in "Elgin Baylor," NBA.

Chapter 4: Jerry West

37. Quoted in Todd Murray, "Jerry West on His Decision to Retire from Basketball," *The Dominion Post*, www.dominionpost.com/af/wvubasketball/stories/2001/03/21/ac/.
38. Quoted in Murray, "Jerry West on His Decision to Retire from Basketball."
39. Quoted in Wolff, *Basketball*, p. 140.

40. Quoted in Bob Carter, "West Was Also-Ran Champion," ESPN,www.espn.go.com/classic/biography/s/west_jerry.html.
41. Quoted in Fred W. Kiger, "More Info on Jerry West," ESPN, www.espn.go.com/classic/add_West_Jerry.html.
42. Quoted in Carter, "West Was Also-Ran Champion."
43. Quoted in "Jerry West," NBA, www.global.nba.com/history/west_bio.html.
44. Quoted in Kiger, "More Info on Jerry West."
45. Quoted in Kiger, "More Info on Jerry West."
46. Quoted in Murray, "Jerry West on His Decision to Retire from Basketball."
47. Quoted in Murray, "Jerry West on His Decision to Retire from Basketball."
48. Quoted in "The Lakers' 'Mr. Clutch,'" Sports Publishing Inc., www.sportspublishing.com/Titles/The-Sports-100-Online/html/Jerry-West.html.
49. Quoted in David Aldridge, "Why Jerry West Was Who He Was," ESPN, www.espn.go.com/nba/columns/aldridge/674251.html.
50. Quoted in Aldridge, "Why Jerry West Was Who He Was."
51. Quoted in "Into the Sunset," *Sports Illustrated*, www.sportsillustrated.cnn.com/basketball/nba/news/2000/08/07/west_retires_ap/.
52. Quoted in "Into the Sunset," *Sports Illustrated*.
53. Quoted in Wolff, *Basketball*, p. 140.

Chapter 5: Kareem Abdul-Jabbar

54. Quoted in "Kareem Abdul-Jabbar," NBA, www.global.nba.com/history/abduljabbar_bio.html.
55. Quoted in Charles Moritz, ed., *Current Biography Yearbook: 1967*. New York: The H. W. Wilson Company, 1967, p. 4.
56. Quoted in Moritz, *Current Biography Yearbook: 1967*, p. 4.
57. Quoted in Moritz, *Current Biography Yearbook: 1967*, p. 5.
58. Quoted in Moritz, *Current Biography Yearbook: 1967*, p. 5.
59. Quoted in Larry Schwartz, "Kareem Just Kept on Winning," ESPN, www.espn.go.com/sportscentury/features/00014022.html.

60. Quoted in Moritz, *Current Biography Yearbook: 1967*, p. 6.
61. Quoted in Springer, *The Los Angeles Times Encyclopedia of the Lakers*, p. 15.
62. Quoted in Zander Hollander, ed., *The NBA's Official Encyclopedia of Pro Basketball.* New York: New American Library, 1981, p. 228.
63. Quoted in Schwartz, "Kareem Just Kept on Winning."
64. Quoted in Wolff, *Basketball*, p. 114.
65. Quoted in "Kareem Abdul-Jabbar," NBA.
66. Quoted in Wolff, *Basketball*, p. 114.
67. Quoted in "Kareem Abdul-Jabbar," NBA.
68. Quoted in Daniel B. Wood, "Kareem Returns to Basketball, Starting Small," *Christian Science Monitor*, www.csmonitor.com/durable/1999/01/05/p1s5.htm.

Chapter 6: Magic Johnson

69. Quoted in "Magic Johnson," NBA, www.global.nba.com/history/mjohnson_bio.html.
70. Quoted in Larry Schwartz, "Magic Made Showtime a Show," ESPN, www.espn.go.com/sportscentury/features/00016111.html.
71. Earvin "Magic" Johnson with William Novak, *My Life*. New York: Fawcett Crest, 1995, p. 15.
72. Quoted in Schwartz, "Magic Made Showtime a Show."
73. Quoted in "Magic Johnson: A Remarkable Court Wizard," Sports Publishing Inc., www.sportspublishinginc.com/Titles/The-Sports-100-Online/html/Magic-Johnson.html.
74. Quoted in Charles Moritz, ed., *Current Biography Yearbook: 1982.* New York: The H. W. Wilson Company, 1982, p. 181.
75. Quoted in Moritz, *Current Biography Yearbook: 1982*, p.181.
76. Quoted in Moritz, *Current Biography Yearbook: 1982*, p.182.
77. Johnson, *My Life*, p. 117.
78. Johnson, *My Life*, p. 120.
79. Quoted in Moritz, *Current Biography Yearbook: 1982*, p. 182.
80. Quoted in Moritz, *Current Biography Yearbook: 1982*, p. 183.
81. Quoted in "Magic Johnson," NBA.
82. Quoted in "Magic Johnson," NBA.
83. Quoted in Schwartz, "Magic Made Showtime a Show."

84. Quoted in "Magic Johnson: A Remarkable Court Wizard," Sports Publishing Inc.

Chapter 7: Pat Riley

85. Quoted in Charles Moritz, ed., *Current Biography Yearbook: 1988.* New York: The H. W. Wilson Company, 1988, p. 480.
86. Quoted in Moritz, *Current Biography Yearbook: 1988,* p. 480.
87. Quoted in Mark Heisler, *The Lives of Riley.* New York: Macmillan, 1994, p. 1 and p. 12.
88. Quoted in Heisler, *The Lives of Riley,* pp. 1, 13.
89. Quoted in Heisler, *The Lives of Riley,* pp. 1, 18.
90. Quoted in Springer, *The Los Angeles Times Encyclopedia of the Lakers,* p. 136.
91. Quoted in Moritz, *Current Biography Yearbook: 1988,* p. 480.
92. Quoted in Moritz, *Current Biography Yearbook: 1988,* p. 481.
93. Quoted in Moritz, *Current Biography Yearbook: 1988,* p. 481.
94. Quoted in Moritz, *Current Biography Yearbook: 1988,* p. 481.
95. Quoted in Moritz, *Current Biography Yearbook: 1988,* p. 481.
96. Quoted in Moritz, *Current Biography Yearbook: 1988,* p. 481.
97. Quoted in Moritz, *Current Biography Yearbook: 1988.* p. 482.
98. Quoted in "The NBA at 50: Pat Riley," NBA, www.global.nba.com/history/riley_50.html.
99. Quoted in "Riley Guarantees a Repeat," NBA, www.nba.com/history/rileyrepeat_moments.html.
100. Quoted in "The NBA at 50: Pat Riley," NBA.
101. Quoted in "The NBA at 50," National Basketball Association, www.nba.com/coachfile/pat_riley/index.html?nav=page.
102. Quoted in Heisler, *The Lives of Riley,* pp. 1, 145.

Chapter 8: Shaquille O'Neal

103. Quoted in Bill Gutman, *Shaquille O'Neal: A Biography.* New York: Pocket Books, 1993, p. 8.
104. Quoted in John Ed Bradley, "Sugar Shaq," *Sports Illustrated,* April 25, 1994, p. 60.
105. Quoted in Gutman, *Shaquille O'Neal,* p. 9.
106. Quoted in Judith Graham, ed., *Current Biography Yearbook: 1996.* New York: The H. W. Wilson Company, 1996, p. 418.
107. Quoted in Gutman, *Shaquille O'Neal,* p. 18.

108. Quoted in Gutman, *Shaquille O'Neal*, p. 58.
109. Quoted in Gutman, *Shaquille O'Neal*, p. 73.
110. Quoted in Gutman, *Shaquille O'Neal*, p. 126.
111. Quoted in Jason Levin, "Measuring Up Shaq," *Basketball Digest*, December 2000, www.findarticles.com/cf_0/m0FCJ/2_28/6715 0662/print.jhtml.
112. Quoted in Levin, "Measuring Up Shaq."

For Further Reading

Peter C. Bjarkman, *The Biographical History of Basketball*. Chicago: Masters Press, 2000. A fascinating look at the history of basketball through the biographies of more than five hundred of the game's most famous and significant personalities.

Gene Brown, ed., *The New York Times Encyclopedia of Sports: Basketball*. New York: Arno Press, 1979. This volume is a collection of articles from the *New York Times* and traces the history of basketball from 1897 to 1979.

Sam Goldpaper, *Great Moments in Pro Basketball*. New York: Tempo Books, 1977. The veteran basketball correspondent presents a look at some of the most memorable teams, players, and games in the history of the National Basketball Association.

Vincent M. Mallozzi, *Basketball: The Legends and the Game*. Buffalo, New York: Firefly Books, 1998. This lavishly illustrated volume pays tribute to three hundred of the greatest athletes ever to play the game.

Robert W. Peterson, *Cages to Jump Shots*. New York: Oxford University Press, 1990. This book examines the early years of the game, up through the first years of the NBA.

Barry Rubinstein, Lyle M. Spencer, National Basketball Association, *The Big Title Champion Los Angeles Lakers: The Official NBA Finals 2000 Retrospective*. New York: Broadway Books, 2000. This book celebrating the Lakers' 2000 NBA Championship contains many colorful photos.

Charles Salzberg, ed., *From Set Shot to Slam Dunk: The Glory Days of Basketball in the Words of Those Who Played It*. New York: E. P. Cutton, 1987. Former players reminisce about the early days of the National Basketball Association.

Works Consulted

Books

Peter C. Bjarkman, *The Encyclopedia of Pro Basketball Team Histories.* New York: Carroll & Graf Publishers, 1994. Bjarkman examines in detail the histories of each National Basketball Association team.

Tim Crothers, *Greatest Teams: The Most Dominant Powerhouses in Sports.* New York: Time, 1998. This volume in the lavishly illustrated series of Sports Illustrated books looks at the greatest sports teams of all time.

Judith Graham, ed., *Current Biography Yearbook: 1996.* New York: The H. W. Wilson Company, 1996. The 1996 volume in the Current Biography series.

Bill Gutman, *Shaquille O'Neal: A Biography.* New York: Pocket Books, 1993. A biography of one of the NBA's best-known famous players.

Mark Heisler, *The Lives of Riley.* New York: Macmillan, 1994. A biography of one of the NBA's all-time leading coaches.

Zander Hollander, ed., *The NBA's Official Encyclopedia of Pro Basketball.* New York: New American Library, 1981. This precursor to *The Official NBA Basketball Encyclopedia* contains statistical records as well as articles on each NBA season.

Zander Hollander and Alex Sachare, eds., *The Official NBA Basketball Encyclopedia.* New York: Villard Books, 1989. This volume contains complete statistical records for every player who appeared in an NBA game.

Earvin "Magic" Johnson with William Novak, *My Life.* New York: Fawcett Crest, 1995. The autobiography of the player who brought "Showtime!" to the Los Angeles Lakers.

Leonard Koppett, *24 Seconds to Shoot.* 1968. Reprinted, Kingston, New York: Total/Sports Illustrated, 1999. This book details the history of the National Basketball Association from its beginning through 1968.

Charles Moritz, ed., *Current Biography Yearbook: 1967*. New York: The H. W. Wilson Company, 1967. The 1967 volume in the Current Biography series.

————, *Current Biography Yearbook: 1982*. New York: The H. W. Wilson Company, 1982. The 1982 volume in the Current Biography series.

————, *Current Biography Yearbook: 1988*. New York: The H. W. Wilson Company, 1988. The 1988 volume in the Current Biography series.

Steve Springer, *The Los Angeles Times Encyclopedia of the Lakers*. Los Angeles: Los Angeles Times, 1998. Printed in celebration of the fiftieth anniversary of the Lakers' franchise, this is an A-to-Z compilation of information on the team, with the emphasis on its years in Los Angeles.

Alexander Wolff, *Basketball: A History of the Game*. New York: Time, 1997. This volume in the lavishly illustrated series of Sports Illustrated books chronicles the amazing growth of James Naismith's sport.

Periodicals

John Ed Bradley, "Sugar Shaq," *Sports Illustrated*, April 25, 1994.

Lee Enderlin, "The Big Number 99," *Sports History*, March 1990.

Ron Fimrite, "Big George," *Sports Illustrated*, November 6, 1989.

Internet Sources

David Aldridge, "Why Jerry West Was Who He Was," ESPN, www.espn.go.com/nba/columns/aldridge/674251.html.

Dan Barreiro, "Before Wilt, Kareem and Shaq, There Was Mikan," *Minneapolis-St. Paul Star Tribune*, www.thesunlink.com/news/99december/daily/1223c1d.html.

"Baylor Hits 61 in the Finals," NBA, www.global.nba.com/nbaat50/moments/baylor_61.html.

Bob Carter, "West Was Also-Ran Champion," ESPN, www.espn.go.com/classic/biography/s/west_jerry.html.

Frank Deford, "A Tiger Who Could Beat Anything," *Sports Illustrated*, March 28, 2000, www.sportsillustrated.cnn.com/features/cover/news/2000/03/27/baylor_deford.

"Elgin Baylor," NBA, www.global.nba.com/history/baylor_bio.html.

"George Mikan," NBA, www.global.nba.com/history/baylor_bio.html.

"Into the Sunset," *Sports Illustrated*, www.sportsillustrated.cnn.com/basketball/nba/news/2000/08/07/west_retires_ap.

"Jerry West," NBA, www.global.nba.com/history/ west_bio.html.

"Kareem Abdul-Jabbar," NBA, www.global.nba.com/history/abduljabbar_bio.html.

Fred W. Kiger, "More Info on Jerry West," ESPN, www.espn.go.com/classic/add_West_Jerry.html.

"The Lakers' 'Mr. Clutch,'" Sports Publishing Inc., www.sportspublishinginc.com/Titles/The-Sports-100-Online/html/Jerry-West.html.

Jason Levin, "Measuring Up Shaq," *Basketball Digest,* December 2000, www.findarticles.com/cf_0/m0FCJ/2_28/67150662/print.jhtml.

"Magic Johnson," NBA, www. global.nba.com/history/mjohnson_bio.html.

"Magic Johnson: A Remarkable Court Wizard," Sports Publishing Inc., www.sportspublishinginc.com/Titles/The-Sports-100-Online/html/Magic-Johnson.html.

Todd Murray, "Jerry West on His Decision to Retire from Basketball," *The Dominion Post*, www.dominionpost.com/af/wvubasketball/stories/2001/03/21/ac.

"The NBA at 50, Pat Riley," NBA, www. global.nba.com/history/riley_50.html.

"Pat Riley," NBA, www.nba.com/coachfile/pat_riley/index.html?nav=page.

"Riley Guarantees a Repeat," NBA, www.global.nba.com/history/rileyrepeat_moments.html.

Larry Schwartz, "Before Michael, There Was Elgin," ESPN, www.espn.go.com/sportscentury/features/00014086.html.

————, "Kareem Just Kept on Winning," ESPN, www.espn. go.com/sportscentury/features/00014022.html.

————, "Magic Made Showtime a Show," ESPN, www.espn. go.com/sportscentury/features/00016111.html.

Stew Thornley, "Game with 12-Foot Baskets," University of Minnesota, www.tc.umn.edu/~thorn017/mplslakers_12foot.html.

Daniel B. Wood, "Kareem Returns to Basketball, Starting Small," *Christian Science Monitor*, www.csmonitor.com/durable/ 1999/01/05/p1s5.htm.

Websites

National Basketball Association (www.nba.com). The official website of the National Basketball Association.

Sports Illustrated (www.sportsillustrated.cnn.com). The official website of *Sports Illustrated* magazine and the Cable News Network.

Sports Publishing Inc. (www.sportspublishinginc.com). The website of Sports Publishing Inc., one of the leaders of popular sports book publishing.

Index

Picture Credits

Cover Photo: © Reuters/Chris Martinez/Archive Photos

©AFP/CORBIS, 72

© Bettmann/CORBIS, 15, 33, 39, 40, 42, 45, 47, 53, 58, 77, 79, 91, 95

Jim Estrin/New York Times Co./Hulton/Archive by Getty Images, 83

Hulton/Archive by Getty Images, 54, 57, 89, 108

© Minnesota Historical Society/CORBIS, 12

© NBA Photos, 20, 29, 31, 43, 50, 65, 69, 71, 82, 88, 92, 105, 107

New York Times Co./Hulton/Archive by Getty Images, 62, 80

Reuters/Colin Braley/Hulton/Archive by Getty Images, 96

Reuters/Gary C. Caskey/Hulton/Archive by Getty Images, 102

Reuters/John Kuntz/Hulton/Archive by Getty Images, 59, 99

Reuters/Sam Mircovich/Archive Photos by Getty Images, 21, 86

Reuters NewMedia Inc./CORBIS, 103

Reuters/Bob Padgett/Hulton/Archive by Getty Images, 84

Sporting News/Hulton/Archive by Getty Images, 7, 11, 17, 24, 26, 28, 34, 37, 51, 56, 64, 67, 68, 75

About the Author

John F. Grabowski is a native of Brooklyn, New York. He holds a bachelor's degree in psychology from City College of New York and a master's degree in educational psychology from Teacher's College, Columbia University. He has been a teacher for thirty-one years, as well as a freelance writer, specializing in the fields of sports, education, and comedy. His body of published work includes thirty-two books; a nationally syndicated sports column; consultation on several math textbooks; articles for newspapers, magazines, and the programs of professional sports teams; and comedy material sold to Jay Leno, Joan Rivers, Yakov Smirnoff, and numerous other comics. He and his wife, Patricia, live in Staten Island with their daughter, Elizabeth.